The Grand Tour

and its influence on architecture, artistic taste and patronage

A series of essays derived from a conference held in Edinburgh
in conjunction with the Royal Society of Edinburgh in September 2007

EDITOR: LESTER BORLEY

EUROPA NOSTRA

Italy played an important role in the Grand Tour, a rather unique experience of life, through which the British intellectual and political elite was formed. Significant reminders and memories of this experience can be appreciated also nowadays, and they continue to offer a unique and important point of reference for those who wish to develop a special cultural and historic link with Italy.

It is particularly significant that the initiative of this publication finds its origin in Scotland, and I am very grateful to the Italian Cultural Institute in Edinburgh and to Europa Nostra UK for their efforts to keep alive such a link, and in response hope that all readers will renew through this publication the fascinating experience of the Grand Tour to Italy.

PIERGABRIELE PAPADIA DE BOTTINI
CONSUL GENERAL OF ITALY IN EDINBURGH

Published by Europa Nostra UK

For Mary
without whom there would be no book

The Grand Tour
and its influence on architecture, artistic taste and patronage

An educational project sponsored by the Italian Cultural Institute, Edinburgh
with the generous support of the Headley Trust, the Leventis Foundation
and the Duke of Buccleuch and Queensberry

Text edited by Lester Borley

Design by Ian Boyter

Printed in Scotland by Allander of Edinburgh

Text set in Bembo

ISBN 978-0-9560657-0-4

Published by Europa Nostra UK

Sources of illustrations are credited throughout the text. All paintings are oil on canvas, except where indicated.
The front cover illustration is of *Colonel Gordon of Fyvie* by Pompeo Batoni
(by permission of the National Trust for Scotland)
The illustration on the back cover is of *Charles Townley in his Library* by Johan Zoffany
(by permission of the Towneley Hall Art Gallery, Burnley Borough Council)

BEMBO: A Classic Typeface

The history of Bembo originates in Venice, an important typographic centre in 15th and 16th century Europe. Many printers established businesses in Venice at this time, but none as significant as Aldus Manutius. Next to Gutenberg, Aldus was perhaps the most influential printer of the Renaissance and the first of many scholar-printers. Late in the 15th century, Aldus published a relatively insignificant essay by the Italian scholar Pietro Bembo. The type used for the text was a new design commissioned by Aldus and cut by Francesco Griffo, a goldsmith-turned-punchcutter.

It seemed appropriate that we should choose Bembo for the text of a publication which further emphasises the impact of Italy on artistic and cultural taste throughout Europe.

FOREWORD

Europa Nostra is a federation of non-governmental organisations and individuals forming a network of heritage professionals and committed citizens who collaborate to protect the natural and manmade heritage of Europe.

The UK members of Europa Nostra meet annually in different parts of the country and choose a discussion topic which is not only relevant to the location, but which also embraces a wider public interest. In September 2007 the meeting was held in Edinburgh, and Europa Nostra UK joined forces with the Royal Society of Edinburgh to organise the meeting on the topic of The Grand Tour and its influence on architecture, artistic taste and patronage. On the previous evening the annual Duncan-Sandys Lecture was given by Sir Timothy Clifford on The Italian Grand Tour and its influence on art collecting in Britain. Other events enabled participants to enjoy the Grand Tour treasures of the National Gallery of Scotland, as well as exploring the neo-classical architecture of the New Town. At the suggestion of the Italian Cultural Institute, it was agreed to publish the papers in order to reach a wider audience, particularly at university and secondary school level.

We are very grateful not only to those who prepared excellent papers for the conference, but also to all those who assisted with other parts of the programme. Owing to their subsequent indisposition, we were unable to include the papers presented by Sir Timothy Clifford and Professor Alistair Rowan in this volume, but we are nevertheless grateful to them for their entertaining lectures.

National Galleries of Scotland gave us wholehearted support, and we enjoyed the generous hospitality of Historic Scotland and the National Trust for Scotland. We are also grateful to the owners and staff involved in the management of Hopetoun House, Penicuik House and Newhailes for facilitating the property visits.

We are grateful not only for the financial support given by the Italian Cultural Institute, but also for that given by the Headley Trust, the Leventis Foundation and His Grace the Duke of Buccleuch and Queensberry. He has always shown a keen practical interest in the educational potential of the treasures collected on the Grand Tour. The illustrations in this publication have been sourced widely from collections in Europe and the United States of America. However we should like to thank in particular the staff of the photo libraries of the National Galleries of Scotland and the National Trust for Scotland. Ian Boyter has produced a most elegant design.

In publishing the papers of the September 2007 Edinburgh conference, Europa Nostra UK will have achieved one of its key objectives, which is to raise awareness among the public at large of the European dimension of our cultural heritage. Whilst many who read this book will never themselves make the Grand Tour, at least they can share vicariously in its pleasures.

Lester Borley

4

Contents

Opposite:

Johan Zoffany (1733-1810)
Charles Townley (1739-1805)
with friends in his library at
7 Park Street *(now 14 Queen*
Anne's Gate, Westminster)
1781-1783

(By permission of the Towneley
Hall Art Gallery, Burnley
Borough Council)

Facing page: Nathaniel Dance (1735-1811) Charles, Lord Hope *(1740-1766)*, The Hon. James Hope *(later 3rd Earl of Hopetoun), 1741-1816*, with William Rouet *(1712-1785)*, their tutor, *1762*

Photo Ian Boyter

Karl Bennert (1815-1885) after Johann Heinrich Wilhelm Tischbein (1751-1829) Goethe in the Campagna *c. 1848. (Original by Tischbein painted 1786)*

(Freies Deutsches Hochstift Frankfurter Goethe-Museum)

François Xavier Fabré (1766-1837) Joseph Allen Smith *(1769-1828)* contemplating the Arno, Florence, *1797*

(By permission of the Syndics of the Fitzwilliam Museum, Cambridge)

Introduction

Lester Borley

The Hopes of Hopetoun were assiduous Grand Tourists over several generations, usually travelling at the age of 18 for study in the Netherlands, augmented by cultural visits elsewhere which could last for 5 years or more. The Hopes retained a sequence of tutors, such as William Rouet, who retired with a well-earned pension. This portrait was commissioned in Rome by the Hope brothers as a gift to their tutor. In a letter home, James felt it necessary to explain why they had employed Dance instead of the fashionable favourite, Pompeo Batoni. "…One Dance, an Englishman, whom we preferred to Pompeo Battoni, because he is reckoned equal in genious and Battoni has as many Portraits for English Gentlemen on hand that we could not expect one for two or three years to come… Dance makes good likenesses and will certainly make a figure when he returns to England".

(By permission of the Estate of the Marquess of Linlithgow)

There are many ways to approach the study of the Italian Grand Tour. In my case, a childhood fascination for the life of Horatio Nelson led me to wonder why he had the title of 'Bronte' after his name. Why was he in the West Indies at one moment and then in the Mediterranean at another? How did he come to meet Emma Hamilton, the discarded mistress of Charles Greville, whose uncle was Sir William Hamilton, the British Envoy to the Kingdom of Naples and Sicily? And why was Sir William more interested in vases and volcanoes than in Emma?

Later, when I was professionally involved overseas in developing themes of cultural tourism for regional economic benefit in Britain, I promoted the remarkable art collections in British country houses to attract visitors. Much later, as a Hopetoun House Preservation Trustee, I passed many happy hours delving in the family papers of the Hopes of Hopetoun, which led me to a letter written by Robert Adam from Rome in 1755, suggesting a design for a fireplace and the name of Rysbrack as a possible sculptor, and so it goes on.

The Italian Grand Tour, which is largely a feature of the 18th century, must be seen in the context of the search for first-hand knowledge which had motivated many travellers in earlier centuries. Albrecht Durer (1471-1528) had travelled to Italy to study the work of the Old Masters, and was particularly impressed by Mantegna in Venice. The scholar and humanist Desiderius Erasmus (1468-1526) of Rotterdam was constantly on the move between universities, developing a network of fellow scholars and intellectuals.

The late 17th and 18th centuries were periods of considerable political and social change and many aspiring public servants, such as Joseph Addison, travelled abroad to study the social and political systems of other nations. Not all Grand Tourists were destined for Italy, and some got no further than the universities of the Netherlands, or even preferred to explore the emerging political structures of northern Europe, particularly Prussia and Russia.

Whilst we have focused in these essays primarily on the British experience of the Grand Tour, there were many other nationalities such as Germans and Americans involved. The 1848 painting by Bennert, based on the original of

1786 by Tischbein, of Johann Wolfgang von Goethe (1749-1832) shows a man of mature years relaxing from his arduous duties for Duke Karl August. He escaped from Weimar to Italy in 1786 and lived incognito for eighteen months, mainly in Rome and Naples. His seminal *Italienische Reise* influenced many of his countrymen to undertake their own *Kavaliersreise*.

The picture by Tischbein of Goethe in the Campagna clearly appealed to Joseph Allen Smith, of a wealthy family from South Carolina, who commissioned François Xavier Fabré to paint his portrait seated on the banks of the Arno in Florence in 1797. Smith was in Europe from 1793 to 1807, largely to form a collection of sculpture for the projected Pennsylvania Academy of Fine Art.

Another person dedicated to art collecting was Charles Townley of Towneley Hall in Lancashire, depicted by Johann Zoffany studying the sculpture collection in his Westminster home, together with Charles Greville and other friends. Townley was a wealthy landowner, but as a Roman Catholic was barred from holding public office at that time, and so he devoted his life and his considerable fortune to the collection of art, visiting Italy several times. He had admired the painting by Johann Zoffany of the *Tribune of the Uffizi*, commissioned by Queen Charlotte for her husband George III. Townley was wealthy enough to be able to commission Zoffany to paint a souvenir of his own Grand Tours.

There are other important examples of Grand Tour collections in many British country houses, such as those described in the opening essay by the Duke of Buccleuch and Queensberry. Another renowned collector was Sir Robert Walpole, the first Prime Minister (1676-1745), who is said to have spent £40,000 (about £5 million at 2008 prices) on his collection displayed at Houghton Hall in Norfolk. It was sold eventually by his grandson in 1779 to Catherine the Great of Russia.

Other royal collectors have included Gustav III of Sweden, whose popular Museum of Antiquities in the Royal Palace of Stockholm houses a collection of over 200 works of art, primarily sculpture, which he collected on his own Italian Grand Tour in 1783-4. The park of the Summer Palace of the Swedish royal family at Drottningholm features a Chinese Pavilion, whose design was influenced by the writings of the Swedish-born Sir William Chambers (1726-96),

Guardhouse, made from painted tin plate, 18th century, for the Chinese Pavilion (below) in the designed landscape of Drottningholm Palace near Stockholm.

Chinese Teahouse (detail) at Sans Souci, Potsdam, near Berlin, 18th century.

(All photos by Lester Borley)

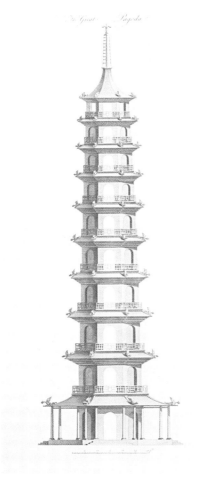

The Grand Pagoda, Kew Gardens (1762)
designed by Sir William Chambers
Watercolour by Tobias Müller

(National Gallery of Scotland)

who, before training as an architect, visited Canton when working for the Swedish East India Company. His books *Designs of Chinese buildings, furniture, clothing, machines and utensiles* (1757) and *A Discourse on Oriental Gardens* (1772) widely influenced the taste for Chinoiserie, particularly for interior design in otherwise austere Palladian buildings.

Frederick the Great (1712-86) built a Chinese tea-house in the park of Sans Souci in Potsdam, and in Kew Gardens one can still marvel at the Pagoda designed in 1762 by Chambers for Augusta, princess dowager of Wales.

The Grand Tour in fact was to influence the ideas of many who had not themselves had direct experience of Italy. This is perhaps most clearly expressed in the ambition of Catherine the Great of Russia (1729-96), born a princess of Anhalt-Zerbst in Prussia. Following the suspicious death of her husband, Peter III, she reigned supreme and set about the Europeanisation of Russia, being influenced through correspondence and contact with many leading European thinkers and writers of the time.

The publication *Baths of the Romans* (1772) by Charles Cameron, an Anglo-Scottish architect who had made the Grand Tour, came to the attention of Catherine. She invited him to St Petersburg to introduce a neoclassical form to her own private quarters, as an antidote to the rococo designs of Rastrelli completed for the Empress Elisabeth at Tsarskoe Selo. Cameron was to spend the remainder of his life in Russia, creating among other things the neoclassical model estate of Pavlovsk for Catherine's son Paul.

Catherine the Great (ruled 1767-95) and Alexander I (ruled 1801-1825) were determined to modernise Russia. This led to the wholesale planning of more than 150 new towns with neoclassical public buildings, designed by William Hastie, the Edinburgh-born protégé of Charles Cameron. When Alexander I visited the Russian Grand Duchy of Finland for the first time he ordered that Helsinki, its capital, be smartened up in neoclassical style.

The Grand Tour to Italy has clearly had a direct and indirect influence on the way we live. The essays which follow amply illustrate the debt which we owe to the rediscovery of the classical heritage of both Italy and Greece.

The monument by Van Nost to the 2nd Duke and Duchess of Queensberry in Durrisdeer Kirk, Dumfriesshire c.1710

Continuing the Grand Tour

Taking Opportunities and facing Challenges on our doorstep

The Duke of Buccleuch and Queensberry

John, 9th Duke of Buccleuch with Rembrandt's Old Woman Reading, *1655*

(All images in this paper by permission of the Duke of Buccleuch and Queensberry)

The recent death of my father, the custodian for nearly four decades of the Buccleuch family collections, casts a sad shadow over participation in this Europa Nostra conference. It remains however a privilege to be able to reflect briefly in this distinguished gathering on the wonderful opportunity private collections, as well as those of the National Trust for Scotland, offer of continuing the Grand Tour here, at home, on our own doorsteps.

The influence of several centuries of Grand Tourism continues to permeate not surprisingly the minds and sensibilities of family descendants. It surely has the potential to reach a far wider audience with its infectious power to enrich across generations and continents.

My father was a fine example of that. Although well known for his concern for rural issues, he was also an extremely well informed and thoughtful steward of his inherited family collections. Yet he had no formal training, but instead benefitted from the osmosis of knowledge accumulated gradually from living with wonderful pictures and furniture, and from discussing and debating with the constant flow of expert visitors. He was determined to share those collections, establishing charitable trusts dedicated to improving the learning opportunities they provided. He loved meeting visitors to his stately homes, and was deeply saddened by the theft of his Leonardo not least because it deprived thousands of people of the opportunity of seeing it. Yet he was no cultural snob and thought the heritage should be enjoyed in the round and in all its richness, seeing in the preservation of a fine mixed working landscape as much value as in the restoration of its complex designed counterpart. In stipulating his burial place in the grounds of the great Cistercian Abbey at Melrose, under the shadow of the Eildon Hills with their layers of Ancient British and Roman archaeology he took conscious comfort from the interweaving of many cultural strands over many centuries.

Easy travel has changed our approach to the way we explore cultures in Europe, and not necessarily for the better. The three days spent with our 15 year old daughter this summer in and around Siena contrasts with the progress of one of my forebears, James Douglas, later 2nd Duke of Queensberry who with his brother William, aged barely 16, and their Tutor, James Fall arrived in Paris in October 1680 at the start of a three year tour that would take them to Siena, south to Naples and then to Venice. Fall's diaries do not suggest they were great collectors. They left Venice 'after we had bought several curiosities proper to the place' which sounds like typical tourist knick knacks. The accounts bear this out – well dressed, well fed, well entertained they certainly were – a guitar is bought and more spent on guitar lessons and lute strings than on a language tutor.

The Castle at Drumlanrig as it is today was commencing construction at the time, a project spanning 20 years, but it is hard to see how it might have been influenced by their travels other than in the horseshoe staircase at the entrance with its faint resonance of Fontainebleau. This was in spite of the fact that the travellers fell in, for their return journey over the Alps and to Antibes, with Louis XIV's celebrated engineer of fortifications, Monsieur de Vauban.

On the other hand, look inside nearby Durrisdeer Kirk, a simple building set in rural isolation in the Southern Upland hills, and you can have no doubt that something rubbed off. The moving tombs of the 2nd Duke and Duchess by Van Nost and its breathtaking marble baldicchino come as less of a surprise when we read the comments by Fall in his manuscript about St Peter's: "the longer we stayed in Rome and the more we visited this Church, the more we

Madonna and the Yarnwinder by Leonardo da Vinci and followers c. 1516

Drumlanrig Castle, c. 1685, in south west Scotland

Boughton in Northamptonshire, showing the North Front and the Stables completed c.1705

The Boughton State Bed c.1680 with the Mortlake tapestries based on Raphael's Acts of the Apostles cartoons

did admire it, till we came to admire nothing else".

My family name is Montagu Douglas Scott, and if we look at the collecting patterns of the English branch, the Montagus of Northamptonshire, there is a much broader link between what we have now and what they saw on their travels. Boughton with its great Versailles style north front with the Mansard roofs was the product of Ralph Montagu's many years as English Ambassador to Louis XIV and then as semi exile in France and in the Low Countries. Thoroughly English it may seem from other angles, with its pitched roofs, courtyards and Great Hall but come inside and you will find the influences in all the decorative arts of a host of craftsmen and artists from the continent led by Daniel Marot. Stars of the tapestry collection which stem from Ralph's stewardship of the Mortlake workshops are the Acts of the Apostles set, themselves the product of Charles I's acquisition of the Raphael Cartoons.

Jump down a few generations and we have perhaps the most identifiable Grand Tourist in the family John Brudenell, Marquis of Monthermer. He too started young, aged 17, but spent nine years away, with the first four in France

where once again there was a problem with language, his Tutor Henry Lyte lamenting his charge's "perseverance in not talking French". He opened his time in Italy with bad notices from fellow travellers – Robert Adam was particularly scathing describing him as "a stupid, meaningless, creature who has not even the mein of as tailor nor the spirit of a louse - and didn't fare much better at the end when on leaving Venice he made little impression on Lady Mary Wortley Montagu who said he was "too indolent to dispute with anybody and appears indifferent to our sex"

On the other hand he brought home exceptional portraits having had himself painted in 1756 in Rome by both Batoni and Mengs, and having travelled right to the very south of Italy commissioned wonderful views by Antonio Joli including Paestum to

John, Lord Brudenell, later Marquis of Monthermer, by Anton Raphael Mengs (1728-79).

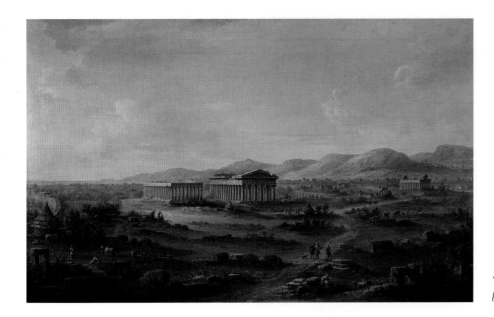

The Greek temples at Paestum,
by Antonio Joli, 1756

which he was one of the earliest visitors. Venice was not wasted either with a collection of Guardis and he also bought for his parents at home several Italian paintings including a ravishing young man by Caracci. Knowing too that he was plagued by the ill health from which he subsequently died at an early age, you can see why his descendants view him in an altogether rosier light.

It was his premature death that resulted in the inheritance by his sister Elizabeth and her husband, Henry Scott, 3rd Duke of Buccleuch of the Montagu collections. The Scott family had been part of Scottish Border history and lore since at least the 12th century. Their homes had been the familiar small fortresses of the border, the simple peel towers like Newark, their title had been earned by an act of opportune bravery in saving the life of Scottish King threatened by a charging stag, an act commemorated many centuries later in a magnificent Garrard candelabra. By the 1760's when the marriage took place they had come a long way from those simple roots. Henry had done a different sort of Continental tour, taking as his tutor, Adam Smith, the man later to become the celebrated economist.

17

Henry, 3rd Duke of Buccleuch by
Thomas Gainsborough, 1768

Notwithstanding a slightly derogatory comment about the merits of the Grand Tour in his Wealth of Nations – 'by sending his son abroad', Smith wrote, 'a father delivers himself at least for some time from so disagreeable object as a son unemployed, neglected and going to ruin before his eyes' Smith remained a life long friend of the young man. They had had in any case an extraordinary two years criss-crossing France meeting people of influence and thinkers including their compatriot David Hume before spending time in 1765 visiting Voltaire in Geneva.

Henry's main home was Dalkeith Palace just outside Edinburgh, built at the start of the century by James Smith, who himself had once been a priest in Rome. In its grounds there is now a fine Adam bridge. In many ways it reflects the influence of travel to Europe and it is amusing to see how it in turn was to influence building on another continent. It was a son of the town of Dalkeith, Robert Smith, who was to emigrate to become one of the leading architects of 18th century Philadelphia, of wonderful churches like St Peters and the historic Carpenter's Hall.

Henry's son Charles also travelled

in Italy in the 1790's although perhaps to less effect. "he has never been well,' wrote Lady Malmesbury, 'since he chose to lay down and sleep upon the hot lava upon Vesuvius. He is a very pleasant, comical young man". It is from then on that we see future generations increasingly captured by what their forbears had seen and acquired. Walter Francis, the 5th Duke exemplifies this tendency to add to and fill gaps in the family collection. It was he who acquired the large Canaletto now at Bowhill because it showed Whitehall and the back of Montagu House in London. He continued to expand the 17th and 18th century French furniture collections, and also the porcelain with a spree of Sevres purchases. Portraiture was almost an obsession, with a particular love of Miniatures more than 800 of which were acquired.

Such acquisitiveness on a grand scale has long since ceased. Today the focus is on conservation and on how this wonderful inheritance can be better seen, enjoyed and understood by wider audiences. Visitors of all ages are welcomed

Whitehall, London, by Canaletto showing the Banqueting Hall and, on the right, the rear of Montagu House, 1752

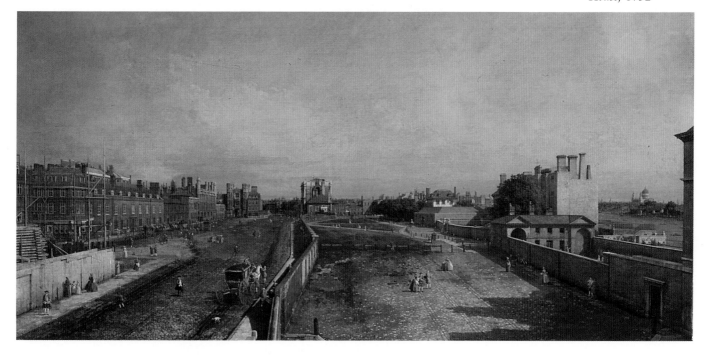

School and university groups studying art are particularly welcomed, as in the Low Pavilion at Boughton, Northamptonshire

in as 'hands on' a way as possible, whether it is children at our Schools Open days wielding a hammer and feeling what the stone mason's skill involves, or connoisseurs for whom silver is brought out to be individually handled and examined in detail. Whilst huge care must always be taken, the learning by osmosis happens because things are used and lived with. The remarkable Chinese style summer house from the 1740's now lives indoors at Boughton, but within living memory it was taken outside to the lawn every summer and no doubt was all the more memorable as a result. I can see it in my mind's eye from early childhood.

But with all this I am still conscious of the extent to which nowadays we tend to skate over the surface in trying to understand such heritage. Most of us lack our forebears' spread of learning, even their inclination to dig deeper into the creative and intellectual processes of artists and patrons in centuries past. For me this is illustrated in my own limited understanding of the evolution of attitudes to landscape, be

A pair of Landscapes by Claude Lorraine 1633, now hung at Bowhill, in the Scottish Borders

it natural or designed. In the Drawing Room at Bowhill hang pairs of Claudes and Vernets and a large Ruysdael. Together they can tell a fascinating tale of different styles and changes in taste in various parts of 17th and 18th century Europe, a tale they carried with them to England and Scotland which surely in turn influenced the managing of estates and the commissioning of designs for landscapes.

It is only now as we embark not only on restoration of our landscapes but on the creation within them of

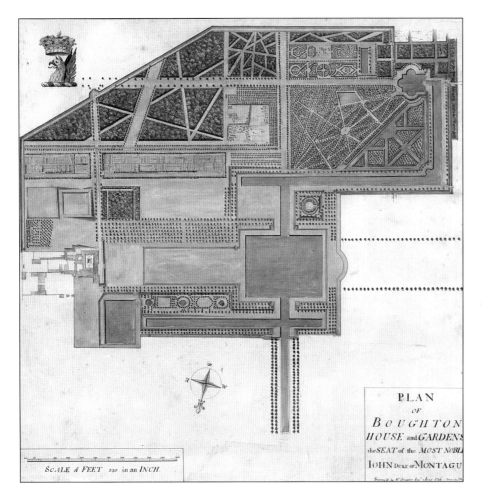

PLAN OF BOUGHTON HOUSE and GARDENS the SEAT of the MOST NOBLE IOHN Duke of MONTAGU

SCALE of FEET 240 in an INCH.

Plan of the Boughton landscape in 1746 drawn shortly before the death of the 2nd Duke of Montagu

visions of our own for the 21st century, that we are coming to see the intellectual forces at work in the past which we must try to match. At Boughton the early 18th century landscape is re-emerging in all its extraordinary and as yet barely understood complexity. To it will be added work by the landscape designer, Kim Wilkie, who has drawn on the Golden Section for guidance for its location and design. Who knows whether our descendants will understand or be interested in that in 200 years time or whether they will just like it for what it is a sunken pool, grassy banks and a spiralling rill and fountain.

Our opportunities for reliving the Grand Tours of the past are clearly there, but how many of us will be worthy of them?

That is the challenge for the future.

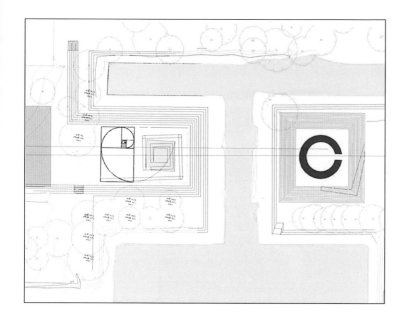

Above, left: 21st century landscape design by Kim Wilkie, for a sunken pool opposite the Mount, under construction in 2008

Left: Students pictured before The West Front at Boughton studying the significance of the cultural landscape

23

*Pompeo Batoni
(1708-1787)*
George Gordon,
Lord Haddo 1775

*(The National Trust for
Scotland, Haddo House,
Aberdeenshire)*

The Grand Tour

An Overview

Patricia R. Andrew

Introduction

The Grand Tour was a phenomenon particularly associated with younger members of the British aristocracy and gentry of the eighteenth century. Although there were earlier antecedents, the custom really started around the middle of the seventeenth century. The classic early guide, which gave the concept its name, was Richard Lassels's book *The Voyage of Italy* of 1670. The Grand Tour was fully underway by the eighteenth century and at its height from the 1740s to the 1790s. It was suppressed during the wars with France, but then had a brief revival in the 1820s before dying out in the age of mass travel in the 1840s.

The British were by no means the only nationality to make the Grand Tour, but they were the most numerous participants and largely set the tone and pattern for travellers from other northern European countries. Immense numbers of young men travelled on the continent for up to three or four years. They enjoyed an experience that was intended to be one of education, cultural improvement, the acquisition of manners, polish and sophisticated taste, though for many it proved to be a mixture of gap year, the expenditure of vast quantities of parental funds, and the liberal sowing of wild oats. It came to be perceived as something of a rite of passage: if a young aristocrat was too poor in health to make the trip, or a young gentleman too poor in funds, he had missed out on both a full education and the all-important activity of purchasing and commissioning paintings, sculpture and books to enhance the family seat, itself frequently inspired by European architectural models. A few more mature Grand Tourists also ventured abroad, having retired from their professions, or leaving their affairs in the hands of agents or adult children. But it was always very much for men. Few women or children came to Italy, and when they did, it was almost invariably to accompany fathers, husbands, sons – or, occasionally, lovers.

In one direction or the other the Grand Tour could take in many European cities. But the focus was always Italy, and the visits to other countries were necessary stages of the journey *to* Italy or the return *from* Italy. Dr Johnson remarked that 'A man who has not been in Italy, is always conscious of an inferiority, from his not having seen what it is expected a man should see. The grand object of travelling is to see the shores of the Mediterranean'.

The naïve and often pampered boys on the Grand Tour were easy targets for critics and satirists. Horace Walpole wrote of 'schoolboys just broke loose, or old fools that are come abroad at forty to see the world'. Robert Burns, the lowly-born farmer poet, described in *The Twa Dogs. A Tale* (1785), the rich young aristocrat abroad, who

...down *Italian Vista* startles
Whore-hunting amang groves o' myrtles:
Then bowses drumlie *German-water*
To make himsel look fair an' fatter,
An' clear the consequential sorrows,
Love-gifts of Carnival Signioras.
For Britain's guid! For her destruction!
Wi' dissipation, feud an' faction!

The Itinerary

In the eighteenth century the journey itself was a formidable undertaking, the many natural dangers compounded by the threats of highwaymen on land and pirates at sea. For the young men concerned, this of course only added to the great sense of adventure. They could make the journey entirely by sea, though most began their Tour in France, and some went south after a period of study at continental universities such as Leiden or Utrecht.

By the 1720s the itinerary had became codified into a set list of expected destinations. For the British, Paris was usually the first main stop, where the tourists would rent apartments for weeks or even months, taking lessons in dancing, fencing and riding, and purchasing fashionable clothes for the next stage of the journey. France was perceived as a very modern state, one that was competing with Georgian Britain, and a great contrast to Italy, which was perceived as a place largely of the past.

In winter the next leg of the journey was often to Lyons and Marseilles, followed by a sea voyage to Genoa or Leghorn; or it might be to Geneva, a safely Protestant city and a good place to prepare for the crossing over the Alps into Italy, an alarming and dangerous experience that was both keenly anticipated and much dreaded. Carriages were taken to pieces and the luggage carried by pack-mules; the wealthier grand Tourists hired guides to carry them on their shoulders in specially-designed chairs. Exhausted, the Tourists spent some weeks of recovery in the north of Italy in cities such as Turin before continuing their journey south.

Timing was important in deciding which city to visit when: there were the Carnivals before Lent in Rome and Venice; Holy Week in Rome; Ascension Day in Venice; and the ceremonies surrounding the liquefaction of the blood of St Januarius in Naples. But the first major stop on the way south was usually Florence, where travellers found a large and friendly Anglo-Italian society, and for much of the century a warm welcome from the British consul Sir Horace Mann. They studied in the Uffizi, an important introduction to the art of both the Renaissance and antiquity. Then they might visit other cities such as Pisa, but many sped directly on to their main destination of Rome (of which more below), where they would stay for some months or even a year or two. Many Grand Tourists then travelled on to Naples, where they would meet Sir William Hamilton, British Envoy to the Court of the Kingdom of the Two Sicilies, a scholar of both classical antiquity and vulcanology (also discussed below). The very adventurous travellers and serious students of antiquity might continue even further, to Sicily or very occasionally to Greece or the Levant.

Returning north, there was an obligatory stop in Venice. It was a magical

Francesco Guardi (1712 – 1793)
The Piazza San Marco, Venice *c.1775*

(National Gallery of Scotland)

place, a cultural link between Europe and the Orient, and a grand stage-set
with its carnivals and pageantry. But it was also the greatest brothel in Europe.
The Scotsman James Boswell was very naughty there, whereas the prim
Edward Gibbon was both amazed and disgusted by the city. Everyone was
captivated by streets full of water. Before the advent of moving film, even the
most accurate depictions failed to explain quite how the place worked.
Professor Adam Ferguson of Edinburgh University, on a very late grand Tour

at the age of seventy, wrote home to his wife in Edinburgh: 'My dear Katey, I am now in Venice… a town built in the Sea & with Streets & lanes paved with Water with Boats for Coaches & Chariots… All this you knew but knowing & seeing I find is different… There are numberless Palaces all of Marble & loaded with ornament but my feeling is not pleasure but Still wonder how the Devil they got there'. Joseph Smith, for many years the British Consul in Venice, was the great patron of Canaletto. James Boswell and the architect brothers Robert and James Adam all left accounts of visiting Smith's palazzo on the Grand Canal to see his collection, later acquired by George III, now one of the glories of the collections at Windsor Castle.

Rome

Up to the 1750s Rome was the goal for most Grand Tourists. They entered from the north through Porta del Popolo, and generally stayed in the area around Piazza di Spagna, a quarter of Rome that became known as the Ghetto degli Inglesi. Rome at this time had little income beyond that drawn in by the Papacy, but the Grand Tourists spent very freely. They employed servants and guides, rented apartments, purchased antique sculpture and Old Master paintings, clothes and accessories, and commissioned 'contemporary' works from artists resident in the city. This led to a huge industry and a large long-term British community. It has been estimated that the British provided the highest proportion of cash income in Rome from 1750 to 1790. We know who stayed where, when, and with whom, as annual census records were made in each parish.

Coffee houses were great meeting places and poste restantes, and the English coffee house in Piazza di Spagna was very much the social centre of artists and guides. One of these – possibly the English Coffee House – is shown in a watercolour by David Allan in the collection of the National Gallery of Scotland. It is worth noting that the term 'English' referred to language rather than nationality. Italians were aware of the existence of Scotland, Wales and Ireland but (as so often today) tended to use the term English for all English-speaking visitors, just as they referred to all German-

David Allan (1744-1796)
A Roman Coffee House *c.1775*
Pen, ink & watercolour over black chalk

(National Gallery of Scotland)

Giovanni Battista Piranesi (1720-1778)
Vedute di Roma
The Tomb of Cecilia Metella
Engraving

(National Library of Scotland)

speaking visitors as Germans. The term they used for the Grand Tourist, so
often an aristocrat, came from the French address for the young gentlemen –
'Milord' – so the young Grand Tourists were referred to collectively as the
young Milordi. The British community split roughly into two distinct social
groups. There were the Grand Tourists themselves and their entourages; and
the artists, architects and antiquarians who came for a period of study, but who
sometimes stayed to make their careers in Italy. The artists provided copies of
Old Master paintings in addition to their own compositions, and they also
acted as restorers, dealers, tutors and guides.

Rome was hugely exciting to these northerners, with its crowds and its
spectacles such as the elaborate public firework displays. The scale and
magnificence of the modern architecture was awe-inspiring. And the ruins and
and archaeological excavations, including the half-buried Forum, were
astonishing. But Rome had become, rather oddly, very much a 'garden' city. It
had shrunk from its earlier size, and cows and sheep now grazed among the
ruins, hence the contemporary Italian name for the Forum, the Campo
Vaccino or 'field of cows'. The crumbling ruins and vast, empty spaces are

John Robert Cozens (1752-1797)
The Colosseum from the North
Pencil & watercolour

(National Gallery of Scotland)

shown in numerous prints made by Giovanni Battista Piranesi (1720-1778). The semi-rural atmosphere of a city full of trees was also enchanting, and recorded as such by artists like John Robert Cozens, for example in his small watercolour of the Colosseum in the National Gallery of Scotland. This strange mixture of sights - the legacy of Rome's ancient grandeur, contrasted with evidence of its downfall and ruin – could cause disappointment as well as awe. James Boswell was shocked to see refuse dumped among the classical ruins, and squatters living in the Colosseum. It was rather disconcerting after Florence, a city much smaller and more manageable in both geography and intellectual scope.

Numerous northerners have left personal accounts of the impact that Rome made on them. The young men on the Grand Tour went armed with an education that included far more knowledge of the classical world than of the contemporary one, and even the laziest knew their Virgil and Horace, and the map of ancient Latium. James Boswell, rather better read than most, was both excited and overwhelmed, and after being guided round Rome wrote 'I was seized with enthusiasm. I began to speak Latin'. One of the most evocative accounts is Goethe's *Italienische Reise* of 1786-7, in which he expresses so vividly the difficulties faced by the serious scholar in dealing with the richness of the cultural experience: 'I have been here now for seven days and am gradually beginning to get a general idea of the city…The most important monuments I take very slowly; I do nothing except look, go away, and come back and look again. Only in Rome can one educate oneself for Rome'; and, 'Wherever I walk, I come upon familiar objects in an unfamiliar world; everything is just as I imagined it, and yet everything is new'.

Tutors and guides, dealers and agents

All the travelling, studying, and purchasing of antiquities by young and inexperienced Grand Tourists required an army of guides, agents and dealers. Many had come abroad with an existing retinue of tutors, chaplains, servants and dogs, but they still needed the services of locally-based guides. Their personal tutors were often known as bear-leaders, a cultural pun on the custom of leading a bear around for money, but here applied to the young British pupils they had to both control and nurture. Some of the guides resident in Italy were early archaeologists and dealers in antiquity. Generally termed 'antiquarians', several were very erudite, such as James Byres (1734 –1817), one of the foremost antiquarians in Rome – indeed perhaps in Italy – and a serious Etruscan archaeologist. Born in Aberdeenshire of a Jacobite family, Byres left Scotland after 1745 and was educated in France. He worked in Italy from 1758 to1790, and contributed significantly to the formation of neo-classical taste in Britain. The Scottish National Portrait Gallery holds a group portrait of Byres with his family and business partner, Christopher Norton, painted in 1776 by the Polish artist Franciszek Smuglevicz.

Franciszek Smuglevicz (1745 – 1807) James Byres of Tonley and members of his family 1776

(Scottish National Portrait Gallery)

Collecting was an important duty for the young Grand Tourists. The business of collecting per se was hardly new, but until the eighteenth century had been largely undertaken through agents and dealers working across Europe rather than by northerners visiting Italy themselves. Many families collected

over several generations of Grand Tours, for example the Hopes of Hopetoun or the Clerks of Penicuik. The Grand Tourists often came with a parental 'shopping list' and sought certain types of items, or paintings by specific Old Master or contemporary artists. There were never enough real antique sculptures to satisfy demand. Copying was therefore quite usual, a typical example being the marble *Venus di Medici* of 1784 by Incenzi Spinazzi (1726-98) in the National Gallery of Scotland. Many antique sculptures were altered in restoration, with missing limbs recreated to complete a piece; this was not perceived as either deception or vandalism in the way it would be today, and the workshops of restorers and dealers such as Bartolomeo Cavaceppi (1716-1799) did brisk business. Visiting students of art and architecture also undertook such commissions for patrons or institutions. The Edinburgh artist Allan Ramsay was asked to buy books for the library of the Faculty of Advocates in Edinburgh. To transport all these purchases there were several British trading houses, such as the house of Aikman, which operated for over a century in Leghorn. Transport could be risky, with theft and piracy a problem in addition to damage from water and careless handling.

Portraits of the Grand Tour

As lasting evidence of their stay, most Grand Tourists had their portraits painted in Rome. There were several portraitists working in the city at the time, including Anton Raphael Mengs and Anton von Maron, but by far the most eminent and prolific was Pompeo Batoni (1708-1787). For nearly half a century he painted over two hundred Grand Tourists portraits, many of them vast, brilliantly-coloured canvases, which have since become *the* images of the British in Rome.

Some of Batoni's portraits show the young Grand Tourist at his most studious, for example *John, Lord Brudenell, later Marquis of Monthermer (1735-1770)*, 1758, in the collection of The Duke of Buccleuch and Queensberry. Most of Batoni's portraits followed a set formula, however, showing a young gentleman leaning languidly against a pillar or other prop, with antique fragments in the foreground and a view of the Colosseum or temple of Tivoli

Pompeo Batoni (1708-1787)
Colonel the Hon. William Gordon
1765-6

*(The National Trust for Scotland,
Fyvie Castle, Aberdeenshire)*

in the background, and often a dog at his feet. Occasionally a young Grand Tourist rebelled against all this: a painting in the National Gallery of Scotland shows an 'anti-Grand Tour' traveller, Alexander, 4th Duke of Gordon, painted by Batoni in 1764. The Duke had paid little attention to the great scholar Winckelmann who conducted him around Rome, and when sitting to Batoni he instructed the artist to make no reference to Italy, so instead we see the Duke engaged in his favourite pastime of hunting. Not surprisingly, when his uncle, Colonel William Gordon of Fyvie, came to be painted by Batoni two years later, he chose to make made a very definite statement about his interest in classical Rome. This portrait, which belongs to the National Trust for Scotland's Fyvie Castle – and which was the image for the Europa Nostra conference – shows a flamboyantly sophisticated Scot, standing beside a marble statue of Roma with a view of the Colosseum in the background. He wears the uniform of the Queen's Own Royal Highlanders, the 105th Regiment of Foot, with the Huntly tartan draped around him in a self-consciously toga-like manner, his hose imitating Roman buskins.

Antonio David (1698-1750)
Prince Charles Edward Stuart *(1720-1788)*

(Scottish National Portrait Gallery)

Jacobites

Rome was the home of the Jacobites, the exiled Stuarts who were claimants to the British throne, dangerous in their political ambition and in their being Catholic. Until 1766 the Stuart court had an official status in Rome and was represented at the Vatican. Because the Papacy recognised the dynastic claims of the Stuarts, the British thus had no formal diplomatic links with Rome for much of the century. However, there was a considerable diplomatic ambivalence based on convenience. The Pope gave personal audiences to important Protestant Grand Tourists, and many Grand Tourists were happy to hire Catholic guides and dealers such as James Byres. After the death of the Old Pretender in 1766, the Pope refused to recognise the claims of the Young Pretender –'Bonnie Prince Charlie' - who was henceforth treated as vaguely-defined and slightly suspect foreign aristocracy. The Protestant Grand Tourists were all keen to glimpse the Pretenders at concerts and in the streets; they had become, in a sense, one of the sights of Rome. There were Jacobite spies aplenty, one of whom may have been the Abbé Peter Grant (1708-1784), a Gaelic-speaking priest who was a support and friend to many a struggling British artist in Rome. Robert Adam mentioned 'dear old Grantibus...a friend who does everything one can desire'. He trained in Rome at the Scots College; his brother Abbé Robert Grant was Principal of the Scots College at Douai. For nearly fifty years he was something of an institution in Rome, an amiable busy-body, genuinely interested in the arts and helpful to young artists, possibly a spy though if so, a remarkably lazy one. The attainted Jacobite Lord Elcho described him as wishing to be 'all things to all men, a Jacobite to Jacobites, a Georgite to Georgites, and an agreeable companion to everyone'. He worked as an antiquarian and guide, in addition to his formal role as Roman Agent (from 1737) for the Scottish Catholic Mission, and he quarrelled with his bishop, who rightly considered that he spent too much time on social activities.

Beyond the cities

Rome, Florence and Venice were essential stops on the Grand Tour, but Italy held a cultural importance beyond its cities in its landscape and rural archaeology, both of particular interest to British Grand Tourists. The idealised concept of this landscape was firmly entrenched in British minds through knowledge and appreciation of classical writings, and enhanced by visual images that had been created by artists of the seventeenth century. Foremost among those who formed their preconceptions was Claude Lorraine (1600-1682), whose paintings, and prints made after them, were much collected by the British in the eighteenth century. Claude's compositions were consciously recreated in the new garden style now known as the English landscape garden. The British even invented the Claude Glass, a convex mirror with which they could view landscapes as if they were framed Claudian paintings. The Grand Tourists were therefore hoping to find in the Italian landscape what they had already seen in paintings – and they were not disappointed.

The 'perfect' Italian landscape for northerners, and certainly the one that became the most quoted 'Grand Tour' landscape view in both literature and visual image, was that of Tivoli, some twenty kilometres from Rome. It had been the location of many country villas of classical times, and the British explored much of this area, both examining and recording the ruins of ancient buildings and the natural beauties of the contemporary landscape. The waterfall at Tivoli, and the so-called Temple of the Sibyl or Temple of Vesta, was included as a backdrop to many portraits by Batoni, and Tivoli temples appeared all over Britain. One example is St Bernard's Well, set on a public path along the Water of Leith in Stockbridge, Edinburgh; it was commissioned by Lord Gardenstone, a distinguished judge who visited Italy in the 1780s. Sir John Soane even built a Tivoli Corner on his Bank of England in London.

At Tivoli also, Hadrian's villa was excavated by the great antiquarian and artist Gavin Hamilton. The Sabine hill-country was of great interest to the Northerners, for this was the area described by the poet Horace, whose work was particularly admired by the British. The Edinburgh painter Allan Ramsay, uniquely for a British artist, made four visits to Italy, over nearly half a century, between 1736 and 1784; the first two were principally artistic, while the latter

Andrew Wilson (1780-1848)
Tivoli near Rome *1820s*

(Collection Iain Gordon Brown)

Pietro Fabris (active 1768 - 1778)
Kenneth Mackenzie, 1st Earl of Seaforth,
1744 - 1781, at home in Naples,
showing (left) the fencing lesson and
(right) the concert party, both 1770

(Scottish National Portrait Gallery)

two were concerned chiefly with antiquarian and archaeological interests, notably with his researches aimed at establishing the site of Horace's Sabine Villa. Newhailes, for whose owners, the Dalrymples, Ramsay had painted several portraits, bears Latin inscriptions over its doors, taken from odes by Horace.

Naples and the South

Moving southwards, the landscape around Naples held more dramatic interest for the Grand Tourist. The setting was both beautiful and dangerous due to a very active Mount Vesuvius. The city itself was a great contrast to Rome, many times larger in its population, indeed one of the largest cities in Europe after London and Paris. It was a bustling, vibrant place, and Robert Adam described it as 'a perfect beehive, swarming with coaches, chariots, shays and people …every large street is in confusion from morning to night'. By the 1750s there was a considerable British presence in the city. One long-stay Scot was Kenneth Mackenzie, Lord Fortrose, later 1st Earl of Seaforth, whose Neapolitan home was recorded in a pair of paintings by Pietro Fabris, now in the Scottish National Portrait Gallery. Naples was a great musical centre and a draw for some Grand Tourists on that account alone, and in one of Fabris's paintings we see the Mozarts, father and son, on their visit to Naples in 1770; Mackenzie has his back to us, while to his left sits Sir William Hamilton, British Envoy to the Court in Naples. Hamilton was a central figure – and welcoming host – to the Grand Tourists over several decades. He was an expert on volcanoes and a great scholar of the antique, keenly following the excavations at Herculaneum and Pompeii; the artist

Jacob More (1740-1793)
Mount Vesuvius in Eruption:
the last days of Pompeii *1780*

(National Gallery of Scotland)

Fabris produced fifty-eight gouache paintings of the area that were subsequently engraved as illustrations to Hamilton's book about the volcanic area around Vesuvius, Etna, Stromboli and the Lipari islands, the celebrated *Campi Phlegraei* (1776). Various painters, such as the Edinburgh artist Jacob More, also recorded the dramatic eruptions, whose enormous *Mount Vesuvius in Eruption; the last days of Pompeii* of 1780 is now in the National Gallery of Scotland. The newly-discovered buried cities of Herculaneum and Pompeii stimulated interest in the real evidence of the antique, and in the development of the neo-classical style. It was all incredibly exciting. When Robert Adam arrived in 1755, he was astonished at seeing 'earthen vases and marble pavements just discovered while we were on the spot', the whole thing 'exactly like a coal mine worked by galley-slaves who fill in the waste rooms they leave behind'.

Joseph Mallord William Turner
(1775 – 1851)
The Piazzetta, Venice *c. 1835*
Watercolour and bodycolour, with pen
and ink and scraping on paper

(National Gallery of Scotland)

The end of the Grand Tour

By the end of the century, few travellers ventured on a journey now made hazardous by the French. By 1793 only around twenty British painters and sculptors were left in Rome. Once French troops entered the city in 1798 the Grand Tour was in abeyance. It was twenty years before travellers started to return in any number. Canova's *Three Graces*, jointly owned by the National Gallery of Scotland and the Victoria & Albert Museum, was commissioned in Rome in 1814 for the Duke and Duchess of Bedford.

Travellers started to return in larger numbers after 1815, and by the mid-1820s the Grand Tour had revived, though it never regained its full momentum and died away with the age of railway travel and its appeal to wider social classes. Like many artists, Turner had to delay his first trip to Italy until 1819.

By 1830 the German writer Heinrich Heine could write: 'Britons are now too numerous in Italy to be overlooked, they swarm across this country…and one can no longer imagine a lemon tree without an English woman sniffing at it.' Ten years later, in 1841, Thomas Cook began his international travel company. By the 1850s, the Edinburgh artist David Roberts reported Rome to be full of foreigners including …'Yankees, with no end of dollars…'. Foreign travel could now be recorded by the camera as well as by the paintbrush. And so the dream of Italy became, in the British mind, a nostalgic collective memory of both the pre-Grand Tour era, and of the Grand Tour itself.

Sources and Bibliography

This article is based on my introductory paper to the Europa Nostra conference, given in Edinburgh on 16 September 2007.

There is a huge literature on the Grand Tour. Many of the diaries and memoirs of those who undertook the Grand Tour have been published or quarried by historians, and most northern European countries now have considerable bibliographies covering their own national experience of the phenomenon. Excellent introductions in English to all aspects of the subject can be found in Christopher Hibbert's *The Grand Tour* (London, 1987), and Jeremy Black's *Italy and the Grand Tour* (New Haven & London, 2003) which is crammed with facts and anecdotal detail. Edward Chaney traces the history of the Grand Tour in *The Grand Tour and the Great Rebellion: Richard Lassels and 'The Voyage of Italy' in the Seventeenth Century* (Geneva, 1985), and in his collection of essays, *The Evolution of the Grand Tour: Anglo-Italian Cultural Relations since the Renaissance* (London, 1998).

Basil Skinner's *Scots in Italy in the 18th century* (Edinburgh, 1966) is the best introduction to the specifically Scottish experience, and an excellent, detailed and scholarly account of the Scots in Venice is provided in Iain Gordon Brown's 'Water, Windows, and Women: The Significance of Venice for Scots in the Age of the Grand Tour' *Eighteenth Century Life*, vol.30, no.3, 2006 (Duke University Press).

An invaluable reference book is John Ingamells's *A Dictionary of British and*

Dr Patricia Andrew

An adviser to heritage organisations on policy development and
fund-raising. She was formerly a
Deputy Director of the Scottish
Museums Council, following an
earlier career as a professional
museum curator in Sussex, Essex
and Durham. Since 2001 she has
been an independent writer and
lecturer on art history subjects,
specialising on the British in Italy
and garden history.

Irish Travellers in Italy, 1701-1800: compiled from the Brinsley Ford Archive (New Haven & London, 1997). Each entry gives details of the individual's itinerary and a list of both published and unpublished sources.

The tercentenary of the birth of the portraitist Pompeo Batoni (1708-1787) has been celebrated with exhibitions in the USA and in London. The accompanying book by Edgar Peters Bowron and Peter Björn Kerber, *Pompeo Batoni: Prince of Painters in Eighteenth-Century Rome* (New Haven and London, 2007), provides both a vivid appreciation of his work and the Grand Tourist experience in Rome.

*Antonia Canova,
(1757-1822)
The Three Graces
(Aglaia, Euphrosyne
and Thalia)*

*(National Gallery of
Scotland and Victoria
and Albert Museum)*

SIR JOHN CLERK, 2ND BART.
Baron of the Exchequer

44

Prelude and Pattern

The remarkable Grand Tour of Sir John Clerk of Penicuik (1676-1755) in the 1690s

Iain Gordon Brown

The destruction by fire of Penicuik House in 1899 signified the end, in physical terms, of the Clerk family's long and intense love-affair with the Grand Tour. Their country seat in Midlothian, some twelve miles to the south of Edinburgh, was the product of an interest in architecture on the part of four successive generations which had culminated in the decision of Sir James Clerk, third baronet, to demolish the old dwelling of his predecessors and to construct to his own skilled amateur design an opulent mansion that would reflect the taste of an owner who had himself spent many years abroad in cultural pursuits, and who had studied architecture and painting in Rome.

In addition to Penicuik itself, the family had once owned the exquisite and influential villa of Mavisbank, at Loanhead, a celebrated house which had been the architectural pride of its begetter, Sir John Clerk, second baronet and the central figure of this most significant of Scottish cultural dynasties, earliest of the Clerk Grand Tourists and principal subject of my paper. Mavisbank had been not only what might be called a laboratory for the villa idea in Scotland, but also a setting for Sir John's collections of art and antiquities, and the focus of his

John Clerk, younger of Penicuik, later second baronet, by Sir John Medina about 1700.

(Clerk Collection, Penicuik).

life as cultural pattern and Maecenas of the day. Sir James's Penicuik and Sir John's Mavisbank were houses directly inspired by Italian models, and were ultimately the most significant material by-products of the Grand Tour experience: the former a splendid Palladian mansion set in a landscape redolent of classical antiquity; the latter (lying rather nearer to Edinburgh) a suburban retreat where *otium* - the pursuit of virtuous, cultivated ease - might offer a release from the *negotium* of public business for an eighteenth-century Scottish lawyer much as it had for ancient Roman magistrate, Florentine Renaissance banker, Venetian senator, or art-collecting prince of the Roman church.

Penicuik and Mavisbank were, and remain, monuments evoking like few others in Scotland the Grand Tour spirit. Gone are the lives that inspired their building as a means of expressing a refined taste formed in Europe and based on subsequent life-long study of classical art and architecture. Gone are the roofs and picture-covered walls beneath and within which the conversation doubtless turned to youthful travels recalled over the claret, or to the expected return of a young man from abroad accompanied by his baggage bearing the cultural spoils of the Tour. Gone are the libraries with their memory-inspiring volumes of travel literature and portfolios of maps. Gone too, at Penicuik, is Alexander Runciman's frescoed vault of Ossian's Hall, that precocious monument of Scottish Romanticism which was the product of the painter's Italian training paid for by Sir James Clerk, a discriminating and knowledgeable patron, who had originally expected to receive for his money and

Penicuik House, from the garden front, showing the arched windows of the library in the attic storey.

(Photo Lester Borley)

Mavisbank, Midlothian, William Adam's published design for the principal front, about 1728, later published as a plate in Vitruvius Scoticus, *Edinburgh 1811.*

patience a cycle inspired by the ancient decorations of the Baths of Titus and on the theme of the *Iliad*.

But, in place of all these things, we have something different, yet every bit as telling. There is an elegiac quality about the gaunt shells of these houses which makes us conscious of the notion of the affinity between their fallen walls and shattered vaults and the very idea of the Grand Tour itself. We may contemplate the ruins of Penicuik, or we may walk on its terraces and admire the sweeping views of an elysium created in deliberate evocation of the literary and mythological landscape of Antiquity, in very much the same way as the designers of that place had themselves marvelled at the real remains of the classical world, as at Hadrian's Villa below Tivoli, or in the Phlegraean Fields near Naples, a numinous landscape redolent of ancient history and legend. In a special sense it is possible to feel that at Penicuik we, too, tread upon what Joseph Addison called 'classic ground', for we can share the experience of men whose lives were profoundly changed by that collision with Antiquity. Their pleasure in the art and learning of the past is now ours, as we study their own history and achievement built upon that culture; and what binds our ages together is the phenomenon of the Grand Tour.

Penicuik and Mavisbank stand as physically silent yet strangely eloquent memorials of the links between Scotland and Europe, especially Italy, in the eighteenth century: two countries in one age joined as never before, or since, by cultural contact and by an almost indefinable bond of sentiment. (Mavisbank may display elements of French and Dutch classicism in its design; but the purpose and feeling of the house is Italian in its inspiration.) Travellers from a cold, remote, poor, narrow, northern land found in sunny, luxuriant, rich, welcoming, bewitching Italy a sympathy both in the past and in the present. Italy was a land not simply of incomparable beauty and a glorious artistic achievement, but it was one possessing an attraction founded ultimately upon ancient ties forged in empire and dominion, and a connection cemented by a common classical education and Renaissance culture. By the time of the Clerks' travelling days, historical and cultural links had come to be reinforced by a peculiar bond resulting from adherence to a faith and a political system which found in Italy (as also, of course, in France, but in Italy the ties seem to have been more enduring) a comfort and security as great as any active Jacobite exile or crypto-Jacobite dreamer could desire.

By great good fortune the Clerk family papers in all their invaluable range and extent, along with the remarkable contents of the Penicuik charter room – a veritable *wunderkammer* such as many a European Grand Tourist might have relished - survived the calamity of the 1899 fire. Those sections of the Penicuik muniments which bear upon the Grand Tour phenomenon, as experienced equally by mainstream family members and by remoter connections in culture and kin, have a special importance. The documents allow us to reconstruct the story of John Clerk's Grand Tour. These sources include: letters to his father and uncles at home in Scotland, and to friends of several nationalities (most met in Holland), many of these letters enthusing about what he hoped to do on the Grand Tour then forming in his fertile, determined and sometimes devious mind; letters from his father, almost invariably hostile to the younger man's (to him) preposterous Grand Tour plans, and fearsome in their severity; fragments of travel journals; accounts for lodging and tuition; lists of his own acquisitions; notes on collections seen; a few topographical and landscape sketches; some rudimentary architectural drawing exercises; manuscript musical scores; and retrospective jottings relating to his own travels, and to travel in general, on which subject he remained a much deferred-to authority, and one prepared to express himself at length on its merits and equally on its disadvantages.

These archival sources can be matched by visual records, the prints and

Openings from the album of sketches by Robert Adam and others, recording views in Rome and elsewhere in Italy.

(Clerk Collection, Penicuik. Photos Iain Gordon Brown).

drawings in the portfolios and plan chests in the charter-room of the present-day Penicuik House, the former stable-block of the 1760s mansion, with its rustic Palladian farm portico, and the distinctly Italian villa-atmosphere about its charming courtyard which makes the modern visitor feel more in Umbria than Scotland. The extraordinary dome which dominates the courtyard near to the charter-room is itself ultimately a link with the world, or at any rate with the mentality, of the Grand Tour and its legacy. Constructed with the utilitarian purpose of a dovecot, this in fact replicates a lost Roman temple of apparently unique type. The prototype had stood, prior to its destruction in 1743, near to the Antonine Wall in Central Scotland, northernmost boundary of the Roman Empire. Sir John Clerk, our great traveller, and some of his antiquarian friends had been interested in this strange reminder of the Roman presence in Scotland. His son and heir, James, constructed the Penicuik replica out of his own antiquarian interest and also as an act, as it were, of filial piety to his father's antiquarian memory. Old Sir John Clerk's interest in the Roman monuments and antiquities of Scotland had grown from his love of classical antiquity developed during his years of formal and more informal education in Europe, whether studying in Holland or travelling in Italy and Southern France. Other antiquaries less fortunate than he had been to have seen the monuments of Rome herself at first hand sublimated their passion for the past by study of the cruder remains of Roman Britain. The discovery of Roman (North) Britain was a domestic development of the Grand Tour spirit and, for Clerk, but one of many ways in which he pursued a 'Roman' life in a Scotland that he sought to make 'Augustan'.

Many of the prints and drawings in the Penicuik charter-room are fragmentary and burnt as a result of

The stable court of Penicuik House, 1763 - 1767. The dome of the reconstruction of 'Arthur's O'on', the mysterious Roman shrine near the Antonine Wall, demolished in 1743, can be seen above the roofs towards the right of the picture.

(Photo Lester Borley).

the fire which engulfed the old house library where they had been stored. But there are miraculous survivals, notably the wonderful album of sketches recording the Italian travels Robert Adam, which volume had come to rest, through the vicissitudes of family connection, at Penicuik, there to be overlooked when Sir John Soane purchased the rest of the great series of Adam drawings which had ultimately descended to John Clerk, Lord Eldin, and which had not found a buyer at the sale of the rest of his vast collection in Edinburgh in 1833.

The paintings in the Clerk collection, as they hang today in the quaintly elegant rooms and corridors of the former stables and estate offices which now are home to the Clerk family, form an important and well-documented assemblage that illustrates in an instructive way how family taste through several generations was inherited but also modified, as the impact of the Grand Tour took hold and affected or altered collecting priorities. We are fortunate in having the picture catalogues and inventories compiled (and constantly updated) by Sir John Clerk, which record what he had inherited from his father and grandfather, what he himself collected in Venice, Rome and Florence, or what he subsequently acquired at auctions or from dealers in London and Edinburgh, and what his son James was later able to buy for the family when that young man, on the loose in Europe with money and no ties, was in a position to frequent the studios of some of the most fashionable Italian painters of the day.

In terms of memorabilia, the family Grand Touring episodes are represented by a host of items gathered in the charter-room cabinet of curiosities. There is the handbook to the varied and exotic collections of the Anatomy Theatre of the University of Leiden, where a ghoulish exhibit (though doubtless fascinating to a young man from Clerk's part of the world) was that described, without further explanation of provenance, as 'the skin of a Scotchman, dried'. There are maps and plans of Paris and Versailles, and souvenir prints – the postcards of the day – of many European sights and cities. There is a portrait print of the Holy Roman Emperor and his Empress, their biographies engraved in minuscule writing forming the endless curls of their wigs, this being a keepsake of John Clerk's time in Vienna when he met the Emperor but probably not for long enough, so to speak, to have read his wig. There are the

John Clerk's travelling medical chest, given to him by the Grand Duke of Tuscany (Clerk Collection, Penicuik) (Photographs: Iain Gordon Brown)

little lacquer boxes containing scores of engraved gems or 'sulphurs' – that is, casts of intaglios – bearing scenes emblematic, mythological or pornographic, carried home in triumph from the wily street-vendors' stalls in Piazza Navona; small slabs of 'landscape' marble from Florence; tesserae from a mosaic pavement in Cicero's villa at Tusculum; the sprig of laurel plucked, in accordance with Grand Tour guidebooks' instructions, from Virgil's tomb at Posillipo, a place of pilgrimage for modern pagans; and there is the fascinating Florentine travelling medical chest presented by Cosimo III, Grand Duke of Tuscany, to his newly appointed Gentleman of the Bedchamber, one Giovanni Clerk, *cavaliere scozzese*, which still retains, in its beautifully fitted miniature drawers, the pills and potions of the seventeenth century pharmacopoeia, the *olio di stomacho* and the tablets individually stamped with the Medici arms.

The two classes of records, the material and the written, come together in one remarkable survival. I well remember my excitement at finding in the charter-room an old, square wooden box. It contained the broken death-mask of Lady Margaret Stewart, and a quantity of her hair. Having married John Clerk not long after his return from the Grand Tour, she had died in childbirth. Her distraught husband had put away these pathetic reminders of his late wife after they had been used by Sir John Medina to paint her posthumous portrait, a picture which hangs today opposite Medina's fine study of Clerk at the time of his being called to the Bar in 1700, an image of a young man polished as few other Scotsmen of his day by his extended European education and travels. But the box contained something else. In one corner I found what looked like a wizened fragment of leather. Attached to it was an old paper label, grimy and scarcely legible, but inscribed in John Clerk's scrawling hand. It read: 'A piece of an old Roman's skin which I cut off a body in the catacombs of Naples in the year 1698 and said to be above 1400 years old.'

It could well be argued that the greatest loss of the Penicuik fire was the pair of stout manuscript volumes constituting John Clerk's travel journal of 1697-99. His was perhaps the most important Grand Tour undertaken by a Scotsman before Lord Annandale in 1717, and thereafter by Robert Adam in the mid 1750s. Although much of what Clerk did can be reconstructed from the sources mentioned above, there would have been no substitute for his own minutely detailed and illustrated record. The fragment, apparently of this journal, which survives, dealing with his time in Genoa on the homeward leg of his tour when he had at last, and reluctantly, turned northwards from Rome, serves to indicate what an important source is now denied to us. 'I do not forget to keep a journal of what is remarkable in the places I come to', the young

traveller had reported to his father in 1697; 'I believe it will turn to a great volume, for I consider everie thing so narrowly that I cou'd almost paint it over easily after I have seen anything.'

From Italy Clerk returned in 1699, on the very eve of the century in which the institution of the Grand Tour came to be formalized or codified so as to adopt the characteristics by which it made such an important contribution to cultural life for those of many nationalities, but for the British above all. I see his experience abroad as being prefatory to the study of the eighteenth-century Scottish love-affair with Europe, and in particular with Italy, as encountered on the Grand Tour in its classic age. So much of what Clerk pursued in the Low Countries, in Germany and the Empire, in Italy and in France, and his thoughts and activities in preparation for that trip which followed on from the years 1694 to 1697 studying law in Holland, may be seen as a prelude to what others of his family, his cultural circle and the travellers of his nation as a whole did after 1700. His experiences form a sort of standard template or pattern against which the achievements of those who came after him may be measured. His Grand Tour pointed the way for a century's encounter with art and Antiquity, with music and manners, with society and politics, with idle diversion and profitable self-improvement. It was on the Grand Tour, and more especially in Italy, that were formed or consolidated the tastes and interests which were to guide him for the rest of his days, and which were later to be diffused more widely in Scotland through his patronage and example.

There is no question that in his Grand Tour – truly the seminal experience of his life – Clerk showed himself at his best: determined, enterprising, courageous, culturally aware, intellectually curious, outgoing and receptive to all that was best in Europe. It is as if he knew that this was to be but a once-in-a-lifetime experience, and that the narrow world of Scotland would close about him to demand upon his return his sacrifice to duty. Perhaps this latterly buttoned-up Scottish Protestant, bred to the arid study and practice of the law, so uncompromisingly loyal to the Revolution settlement, an architect of the Treaty of Union, and a staunch defender of the House of Hanover through successive Stuart alarums and excursions, might really have been happier, when young and untrammelled, to have remained in Rome as the Catholic Jacobite

An allegorical representation of the idea of the Grand Tour and its role in the cultivation of the arts, from Alexander Drummond, Travels though Different Cities of German Italy, Greece and Several Parts of Asia... *(London, 1754).*
Engraving

(National Library of Scotland).

53

exile towards which crepuscular existence some of his Grand Tour adventures do actually seem to point the way. But then the whole Grand Tour phenomenon was peculiar: immature boys catapulted from the humourless, art-starved, Calvinist prejudice of Scotland to the seductively sinful pleasures of Venice in her long decline, the heady opulence of the counter-Reformation art of Baroque Rome, the soft luxury of Naples and its delicious bay, or the arrogant grandeur of Versailles in its *ancien régime* noon-tide. In his reaction to these conflicting emotions, as in so much else, Clerk's experience was indeed a prelude and pattern.

The Grand Tour, particularly in its Italian manifestation, inspired by turns loathing and longing: the divide is usually one between generations, given added piquancy in the 1600s by religious fear and prejudice, and, in the 1700s, by concerns over morality, extravagance and patriotism. The well-known adage 'An Englishman Italianate is a devil incarnate' may represent one side of the long-running argument. But the fact was that, even by the end of the seventeenth century, and even in remote Scotland, something approaching Samuel Johnson's later celebrated dictum was beginning to have currency: that a man who had not been in Italy was always conscious of an inferiority. Nevertheless, when Clerk went abroad, for every father who held, with Lord Shaftesbury, that, by travelling, their boys might be 'polished by degrees into a general and universal humanity', there remained far more who feared, with John Locke, that the Grand Tourist was fated to pick up irreligion and atheism along with his other curiosities and show them about on his return as choice acquisitions. It was argued that dabbling in 'antiquity-study' inclined a man to popery. As late as 1780, a mob protesting at the Catholic Relief Act threatened to burn Penicuik House because Sir James Clerk had a portico with columns adorning the mansion that held his father's collection of – horror of horrors – *Roman* altars, and that he must therefore clearly be either a papist or a 'favourer'.

The Clerks of the seventeenth century were familiar with northern France and the Low Countries. Trade and cultural connections and some modest taste for adventure took them thither, and rendered those parts of the Continent acceptable. Our John Clerk's grandfather, an enterprising merchant in Paris with a specialist art-dealing business, had acted as a 'furnisher' for young men

Sir John Clerk of Penicuik, first baronet, about 1700 by Sir John Medina.

(Clerk Collection, Penicuik).

travelling in Europe: he disbursed money, and handled their bonds and debts while abroad. Man of taste or not – for this *marchand amateur* grew to love the goods he dealt in for their own sake, and became a full-blown connoisseur in his own right – John Clerk the agent had definite ideas as to where young men might travel with minimum danger to their souls or prejudice to their pockets. Italy was anathema. Of a young man whom, in his role a banker and minder, he was actively trying to dissuade from travel to the south, Clerk wrote that he had 'used all imaginable means to detain your bro[the]r fra that Italien voyadge which wold have proven dangerous, expensive & no wayes proffitable'. Clerk, the merchant-connoisseur, may have founded both the family fortunes and the family tradition of European contact and adventure, may himself have travelled widely in northern Europe in the course of his business, and may have been the great artistic progenitor of a family intimately associated with collecting and the arts; but his animus against Italy, so far beyond the pale, would have to wait another two generations until it was spectacularly overturned by his grandson, in whom a taste for Italy and its art, architecture and landscape overtook and displaced the Northern preferences he had inherited. In turn his own brothers, cousins and sons would likewise gravitate there.

Our John Clerk's father, the first baronet (created so in 1679), confessed that he had toyed with the idea of seeing Italy in his youth, but that paternal pressure, and his own recollection of religious duty, had dissuaded him. He never dared to look southwards again, believing that across the Alps lay damnation and spiritual, moral, physical and financial ruin. So great and so vehement was this suspicion, amounting to fear and even loathing of Italy, that one wonders whether the art-dealer and his grimly Calvinist son could not trust themselves *not* to fall under her spell. Paradoxically, they contented themselves by hanging Netherlandish Italianate landscapes and mythological scenes upon their walls. When our John's father did go abroad briefly in 1676 (the year of his son's birth) is was on a restricted circuit, a variant of what was sometimes known as the Little Tour. He visited Paris, where he made some study of science and architecture, and then progressed though Flanders and the Netherlands, largely to familiarize himself with the military arts in this, the cockpit of Europe. All the evidence suggests that this was a pretty serious-minded venture; but in later years, when he came to record some retrospective autobiographical notes, perhaps about the time that the past came back to him when his own son was rapidly going (as he believed) to the dogs in his determined rush down the road to Rome, he declared that his own trip had been made simply to seek his carnal pleasure and indulge his transient curiosity. Both these commodities would, of course, become fairly standard elements of the classic Grand Tour of the eighteenth century, as contemporary record and later historical prurience would have it.

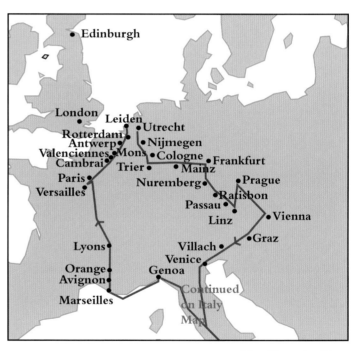

Maps illustrating John Clerk's European travels, 1697-99, beginning and ending in Holland (the Italian section being shown in greater detail).

The first baronet of Penicuik was violently opposed to John's mad desire (as he saw it) to go to Italy. One can almost hear the rising crescendo in his voice as he wrote this letter. 'Our young nobilitie and gentrie by yon travelling abroad acquire nothing but a devilish dexteritie of atheism, sensualitie, vanitie, idleness, and prodigalitie and when they come home either plye themselves to nothing or to nothing that's good… and do live here many years a sad, disgusted and melancholious life… All which flows from the mean companie of fencing, dancing and ryding, singing, drolling and bawdie, poor and vaine masters and companions which young sparks for the most part either must or do choose.'

From childhood John had been fascinated by classical antiquity. Study of Greek and Latin at Glasgow University followed. To Leiden he went to pursue the Dutch legal training then thought desirable for a career at the Scottish bar. But at Leiden, too, he became determined to acquire the widest possible virtuoso culture, and he saw that travel was the most effective key to that end.

On this point father and son parted company, and the divergence of outlook drove a wedge between them. Damning, implacable parental opposition was to overshadow young John's time in Europe in the years after Holland, and the consequences of the episode lasted long. The misery of this coolness, compounded by the crippling debt secretly incurred through prodigal over-extension of time (and therefore of over-spending) in Rome, must often have seemed akin to some form of divine retribution for the wilful indulgence of his

own pleasure as matters weighed upon him in the years after his return to Scotland. It is a fact that his expenditure on the Grand Tour directed the future course of his life, in that it determined his choice of specific career-moves in politics and the law. It is not too much to say that the Treaty of Union between England and Scotland of 1707 is due in some slight measure to the cultural extravagance in Europe of John Clerk, younger of Penicuik, a Commissioner for the Treaty, and who accepted the task with an eye to a future clear of Grand Tour debts!

It had been understood between father and son that some limited form of short Continental tour would in all probability follow on from Leiden, by way of adding polish and a little knowledge of the world: the Low Countries and northern France, but most emphatically not Italy. Yet in young Clerk's sights was this very land, and with that change of inclination the opportunity to gain a knowledge of antiquities, art, architecture and music that would overtake the more limited preferences of his forebears. Few Scotsmen of his day or indeed for years afterwards would return home with quite such wide travelling experience or range of intellectual contacts as he was to enjoy.

When John Clerk made his European travels, he was embarking upon a recognized stage in a well-to-do young man's educational development. For the Grand Tour as a distinct social and cultural episode had become an established institution even before Richard Lassels, in *The Voyage of Italy* published in 1670, had given the concept a lasting name. In their cases for and against Italian travel, Clerk and his father encompass all the arguments on that subject which headstrong sons and fearful fathers had been expressing throughout the century, ever since 1642, when James Howell had written the first travel handbook in praise of 'Peregrination, which therefore may be not improperly called a moving Academy'. The idea of travel as an essential part of the education of a gentleman was further codified by Lassels; and it is his words that best epitomize Clerk's own motive for seeking to illuminate his Leiden studies by travelling. 'No man', Lassels declared roundly, 'understands Livy and Caesar like him who hath made exactly the *Grand Tour* of France and the *Giro* of Italy.'

Italy was the ultimate goal of the full-blown Grand Tour, and the routes to it various. The typical Tour consisted of a common minimum experience which was a round of Paris and some other localities in France, mostly lying on routes to or from the Mediterranean coast, and as many of the sights and sites of Italy as could be managed, of which Venice and Rome were mandatory, Florence desirable and Naples a steamy treat on the side. Innumerable variations were possible on the outward and homeward legs of the journey to Italy, depending on the clockwise or anti-clockwise direction chosen, the time and money available, and external factors such as war and plague. An ideal itinerary would build round the Tour's essential armature some acquaintance with other cities of France; possibly the Ligurian shore and, or alternatively, the 'horrid' experience of the mountains of Switzerland; Vienna, with perhaps a foray into Hungary; the smaller courts of Germany such as Leipzig, Dresden, Frankurt and Dusseldorf; and the great cities of the north such as Antwerp or Amsterdam, for it was in Holland that many Scottish Grand Tours began, since these journeys were frequently extensions of a period of study of law or medicine at the Dutch universities.

Clerk had left for Holland fortified by a quantity of paternal advice designed to guide him though the Leiden years and whatever short period of travel might follow. He was to be aware that this time might 'according to your good or bad improvement thereof prove either exceedingly advantageous or disgracefull and ruining'. He must 'shun whoredom, drunkenness, squabling, dycing, carding and such who use those abominations as hell.' He must avoid

John Clerk as a student at Leiden, a drawing by Willem van Mieris.

(Clerk Collection, Penicuik. Photo Iain Gordon Brown).

Herman Boerhaave's striking monument, designed by Frans Hemsterhuis, c.1760, with a motif of youth and age, in the Pieterskerk, Leiden, Netherlands.

(Photo: Iain Gordon Brown).

contact with flashy women – 'bonie well-dessed up beasts' – and eschew 'fools and chyldish blades'. He must avoid (but tactfully) contact with Scotsmen, for talk of home and a feeling of camaraderie might interfere with hard work. One piece of advice that certainly indicates no willingness to comprehend the demands of an extensive travelling education, and which conveys the expectation that the boy would spend most time at his books, was his father's reminder that 'a sedentary lyfe requires little feeding', thus hinting at a hoped-for economy. Finally there was the very Scottish caution: 'Be not tinkling siller in your poutch or taking out four or five guineas to pay a halfpenny loaf, as some vaine emptie fools do.'

Young Clerk's turning towards a virtuoso life at Leiden provoked anger and anxiety on the part of his father. 'You were sent by me to Holland', the baronet fulminated, 'to studie not architecture, nor policie nor fidling nor to see curiosities for that is not deutie, but to study law.' The youth was devoted to mathematics, and even this was too much for his father. 'The Italians call a fool a little mathematician, and I hope you're not so great a foole as to aime at being a famous one.' The Italian jibe must have been made in the consciousness that, little by little, the Italian design was being worked into the fabric of the younger Clerk's European education. Inspired by the teaching of the great Dutch scholars in Roman literature and history, Perizionius and Gronovius, he became more and more enthralled by the ancient world, and it was natural that he should seek to visit Italy to see for himself the material remains of the civilization he had read of in books. He took lessons in drawing from Willem van Mieris in preparation for a tour that would need to be recorded not only in verbal but also in visual memorial. The greatest of his virtuoso inclinations at Leiden was music, and Clerk became prominent in a 'conventiculum musicorum' which had adherents in Germany and above all in Italy. Clerk's closest friend at Leiden, music uniting them, was the great physician Herman Boerhaave, whom he introduced to porridge. In their Latin correspondence Boerhaave pronounced this, when eaten with cream, to be 'nutrimentum divinum'. Perhaps to these classicists it seemed like ambrosian food of the gods.

Clerk's father, at that time engaged in buying land and coal mines, was outraged when the request came for permission to make the *giro d'Italia*. There was no money 'to throw away' upon such a jaunt, as the young man in his 'madness' seemed bent on doing. For every one who received advantage by a journey thither, a thousand were ruined: 'there are none go there but either such who studie politicks or such who study sensuality and carnall pleasure, those arts being furnished with the best professors in the world at Rome… the place where Satan hath sett up his throne conspicuously' and where there were 'strumpets and whores as numerous as attoms… If a man would be an atheist and a gentile well-bred devill, lett him go first to Rome and second to Venice.' For Sir John, the study of Roman history in the library was acceptable; but 'to have deep impressions of *novum* and *vetus Latium* and of *Roma subterranea*, and as to the old ruines and new buildings thereof is most distracting, diverting and useless, and what pains I have tane that way I look on as lost…' John's 'frolic letter' stating his burning desire to go to Italy – 'If I had 40,000 pounds in my pocket', he had written dramatically, 'I wou'd throw it way to have libertie to go there' – was answered by the dire threat of disinheritance. John would be condemned to live 'as a beast

voyd of the fear and love of God' to follow his 'sinful appetite in so far as your purse will reach…' In answer to this tirade, John now stated his sincere belief that 'ther is no wonder bot a man who loves the Roman storie will have as great a desire to see its Monuments as a Jew wou'd have if the Temple of Solomon were standing to this day.' He argued that in architecture and painting 'all the world are bot imitators of the Italian masters'. His education was such that it had bred admiration in him for what he now wanted to do and to see and to learn more deeply. 'I have verie good grounds to believe', he concluded calmly, 'that a man, if he make the right use of it, will be far the better by an Italian journie than any other else…'

Richard Lassels had stressed the importance of a dependable travelling tutor or so-called bear-leader of the kind that, in our John Clerk's lifetime, Scotsmen like James Hay would become. Clerk's merchant grandfather had played something of the role in his function of disbursing money to travelling young men, and watching and reporting back to Scotland on how it was spent. However, as agent of parental disapproval and expresser of concern to travellers or would-be travellers he was perhaps more of a bear-restrainer than bear-leader. Our John was confident of his ability to make his way alone, without either governor or companions. Unlike Lord Balvaird, for whom Lassels had written an early version of his *Voyage of Italy* (the manuscript is in the National Library of Scotland), he had no experienced tutor to present Italy (in Lassels's delightful culinary metaphor) 'carved and cut up to his hand', but had to 'fall upon the whole joints' of the country himself and serve his own meal. For a young man of enterprise and spirit this was arguably an advantage. Such was John Locke's opinion; and Clerk's experiences support the philosopher's view that a bear-leader sheltered his charge excessively and prevented him making his own way in the world. 'I ask', wrote Locke, 'amongst our young men that go abroad under tutors what one is there of an hundred, that ever visits any person of quality? Much less makes an acquaintance with such from whose conversation he may lean what is good breeding in that country and what is worth observation in it… For men of worth and parts will not easily admit the familiarity of boys who yet need the care of a tutor; though a young gentleman and stranger, appearing like a man, and showing a desire to inform himself in the customs, laws and government of the country he is in, will find welcome,

An evocative etched view, heightened with white gouache, of the colonnade of Piazza di San Pietro, Rome.

(National Library of Scotland).

61

assistance and entertainment everywhere.'

John's remarkable social success, and with it access to the art-collections and *conversazioni* of a grand world, was founded on an easy nature, keen intellect and an uncommon musical ability. He took part in concerts and operas in the courts of Germany, and looked at pictures and observed ducal manners the while. At Vienna he was received by the Emperor, with music as the mutual connection. The audience was conducted in the language of opera, Italian. Clerk confessed that he had spoken as best he could, for 'I was in great confusion, having never been used to talk to so great a man… After I was come out, and considered how humbly and discreetly the Emperor had been pleased to speak to me, I could hardly believe it to be anything but a dream.' However he recovered his composure and down-to-earth Scottish common sense sufficiently to write subsequently of Leopold as 'a very little man, with the uggliest face in the world', surely an amusing combination of the traditional Scottish attitude of 'I ken'd his faither' with recognition of a Habsburg's natural place in the international good-looks stakes.

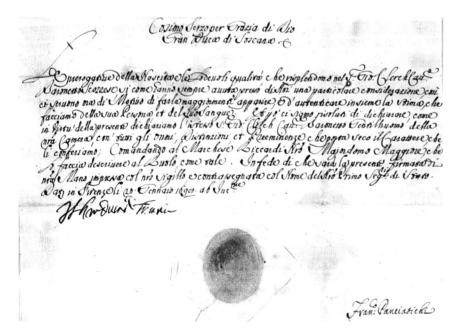

Patent appointing John Clerk a Gentleman of the Bedchamber to the Grand Duke of Tuscany.

(Clerk of Penicuik Muniments, National Archives of Scotland).

Clerk frequented intellectual circles in Florence, becoming acquainted with the eccentric librarian Antonio Magliabecchi, a man even uglier than Leopold of Austria. In Florence, too, as we have noted, he became a member of the household of the Grand Duke of Tuscany, and Cosimo had earlier made an unsuccessful effort (or at least John said he made an effort) to have him squeezed into some vacant Medici apartment at Trinità dei Monti in Rome. The failure of this plan was excused on the ground that the rooms would not have been good enough for one of his quality. In Rome he kept company with cardinals and contessas, and moved in a glittering world of princes and palaces which extended to seasons of *villeggiatura* in the Castelli Romani. Prince Pamphilij, the Strozzi family and Cardinal Pietro Ottoboni, Papal Secretary of State, were his particular acquaintances. His intellect was honed in the company of Monsignor Chiampini and his Accademia Fisico-Mathematica, and he appears to have been connected with the celebrated Accademia degli Arcadi. At Naples he was on terms of friendship with several English noblemen then on tour. At Genoa he tried his hand (and just possibly other parts of his anatomy) at becoming *cicisbeo* to an aristocratic lady, but seems to have stopped short of the kind of serial amorous intrigue without which most Grand Tourists would have considered an Italian trip woefully incomplete. And yet his father continued to believe that young men never met any persons of quality on their travels, and that it was difficult to come into contact with the right company: 'this no man in Scotland can pretend to or promise in his travels, and far less my sone.' In this aspect of his tour, as in so many others, young Clerk was to prove his father utterly and gloriously wrong. He was able to report to Sir John, as part of a lengthy process of self-justification both of prodigal expenditure and prolonged residence abroad, that reports of his social progress were not entirely exaggerated, and did him no disservice, 'since that whereas other people never saw anything but the walls of the towns I can at least show that I not only saw the greatest people there but was intimate with them…'

Intimacy of another kind was skilfully and genteelly avoided when, on a storm-tossed, corsair-threatened coastal voyage by felucca from Genoa to Marseilles, and in the intervals on shore, a fiery young Spanish lady, 'lewd' and 'frantick' as Clerk recorded, took 'more than ordinary pains to make me one of her gallants'. Recently married, her hot-blooded husband was madly jealous:

his officer's sword and her nymphomaniac 'follies in the Spanish way' threatened both our virtuous Scotsman's life and morals, and the fury of the sea menaced boat and passengers in a classic Grand Touring travel-danger episode of the kind that young Allan Ramsay would experience in the 1730s, and without which no European adventure was quite complete – if, that is, one lived to tell the tale at home afterwards.

What a man tells us he did, and what actually happened, may be two different things. In the circumstances of the Grand Tour – activities pursued at a distance from home in conditions wholly unlike anything experienced in earlier or probably, indeed, later life – it is always difficult to know what or what not to believe. In a letter of the time Clerk told his father that he had been to Prague. But he never mentions this Bohemian diversion in his autobiography, and there is no other evidence to support his contemporary statement, which I suspect may have been a subterfuge to mask time (and therefore money) spent elsewhere, possibly in Venice – and there possibly masked; and we may share Dr Johnson's surprise that a man who had been to Prague should keep silent about it.

A number of reasonably impartial accounts of Clerk's conduct do, however, survive. A Jacobite exile, Father James Forbes, reported on the progress of 'young Pennykook', who 'had enjoyed all the honors and satisfaction which once noblemen of the best quality could have expected. It is truly his sweet and obliging humor has made him deserve all these favors, even of strangers…' The Jacobite element here is interesting and important, for it anticipates one of the great themes of the eighteenth-century Scottish association with France and Italy. Many Scots in Europe played a double game, ostensibly loyal to the outcome of the Glorious Revolution and the Hanoverian Succession yet secretly dabbling more or less seriously in the murky waters of Jacobite intrigue. The story of Clerk's success in Rome is intimately associated with the activities of two mysterious Scottish Catholic agents, *éminences grises* who themselves prefigure in some ways the life and motives of the celebrated Abbé Peter Grant in the middle years of the eighteenth century. Clerk's father would have been horrified had he ever known the full story of the company his son kept in the Eternal City with the eternal enemies of King William. It was enough that he was a favourite disciple of old Monsignor Caprara of the Rota

XXVIIII

A Grand Tourist rides at Lake Avernus, a view by Pietro Fabris from Sir William Hamilton's Campi Phlegraei *(1776).*

(National Library of Scotland).

Romana, the Vatican court, probably not something to boast of when back in Parliament House in Edinburgh and seeking admission to the Faculty of Advocates. But to have been the pawn of not one but two Scottish priests, one a Jesuit, who may or may not have been distant kinsmen, was pushing his luck. It says much for Clerk's family loyalty, if not his grasp of the hard realities of the search for political and legal advancement in the Scotland of the early eighteenth century, that he was still keeping in touch with one of these characters many years later when the priest was in Spain and Clerk himself was a baronet and a Baron of the Court of the Exchequer in Scotland who was constantly hoping to be appointed by Walpole head of that branch of the law. And was it not a little surprising that Clerk should purposely have visited Loreto, scene of so much Catholic credibility, and been nursed back to health by nuns in the Roman convent of the Tor de' Specci?

Of course it may simply have been interest in art, architecture and Italian landscape that took him to such places. The Holy House of Loreto was an exquisite piece of architecture as well as a monument to gullibility and the Roman Church's greed. Certainly devotion to pagan literature and mythology was the principal attraction of Naples and the Phlegraean Fields. The memory of the numinous grotto of the Sybil at Cumae remained with him to inspire, years later, the building of his own cave and secret place of contemplation at Hurley on the Penicuik estate. Italian painting and architecture likewise continued to influence his taste. In Rome, where the very fabric of the city was the most enjoyable and instructive of textbooks, to be assimilated in the course of an agreeable walk, he had engaged a teacher of architecture, and he studied painting in the circle of Carlo Maratti. His didactic poem of the 1720s, 'The Country Seat', is full of allusions to the 'un-exhausted stores, the surest

The Villa Almerico (Rotonda) at Vicenza, later the Villa Capra by Andrea Palladio.

(Photo: Iain Gordon Brown).

rules' without an understanding of which, from Vitruvius to Palladio, the modern architect could offer 'no pretence to understand Architectory'. The imaginary mural decorations and the desirable easel paintings that would, in the poem, ornament his ideal royal palace or house of state would also, of course, be brought from Italy, or be inspired by decorative schemes familiar to him from Venetian or Roman palaces. Very soon after his return to Britain, Clerk came to be regarded as an authority on all such matters, and this deference to virtuosoship, *ex Italiae*, lasted all his life. His son James was to be so impressed by Rome, and so much influenced by his father's experience of and devotion to Antiquity, that in the 1760s he would design (though alas not execute) a splendid library (with a Turkish bath in the basement) modelled upon the Pantheon, complete with (and completely in disregard of the Midlothian climate) an open *oculus* in its coffered roof.

Genoa, thought Clerk, boasted the finest palaces in the world. The memory of these outlasted those of the mysterious Genoese lady's charms. It was the libraries and galleries that he most remembered in Florence, where he undertook serious study of old master prints, and where he bought a fine late-Baroque terracotta *modello* of Ganymede and the Eagle. If his father had marked down Venice as a place of particular moral danger, he need scarce have worried. The Bibliotheca Marciana rather than the ridotto and the boudoir claimed his son's attention, and incunables rather than the infamous courtesans consumed his time. Palladian villas on the Venetian *terraferma* introduced him to the villa idea not simply in purely architectural terms as a building type, exquisite and compact, but as a locus for a way of life. At Venice music and painting were enjoyed and studied: not just Tintoretto and Veronese, but also the young Rosalba Carriera, whose pastel portraits would soon be the hallmark souvenir of a visit to *La Serenissima*. In later years he would re-appraise his Rosalba purchases, annotating a picture inventory with the comment about these chocolate-box images of Venetian girls that there was 'nothing remarkable in them'. For Clerk, Venice perhaps represented the more transient glamour of the Grand Tour, and the element that most easily vanished when one came down to earth again in stern, Calvinist Scotland.

Rome, by contrast, was to remain with him for ever. It represented the absolute city, so that when he came to know Paris towards the end of his European travels the sense of anticlimax was profound. He assessed the city, and especially Versailles, as a 'compend of all the splendour and vanities of the world'. Louis Quatorze, whom he saw, was characterised as 'a big, black, sensual man', 'always under the Government of some Woman or other, and vastly intoxicated with the flatteries of those about him'. So much for *le roi soleil*. All seemed but a mean copy, an awkward imitation of the originals he had observed with such pleasure and instruction in Italy – palaces, gardens, villas, fountains, statues, paintings. Clerk whiled away his Paris time studying mathematics with a Scotsman. He wearied of everything but dancing, so that the greatest encomium he could bestow upon a Frenchman, he wrote, was that he was a good dancer. Clerk waspishly noted that neither Spaniards nor Italians would credit the French even with this talent, nor 'any other agreeable gesture or mein but what became a Monkey more than a Man.' Perhaps concerned that Paris was, after the experience of Rome, merely a time-wasting, trifling sort of place, he hastened to reassure his father that he would not appear the fop which clearly the baronet feared. 'At my coming home I do not doubt but you will expect to see a travelling Rhodomontado… or French Monsieur, but I'll assure you of the contrarie, which I hope you shall find. Here in France I might lairn some litel fopish divertisments as dancing, etc., but because my talent does not lie that way, I shall rather lairn to be what they call un Galant homme than un homme Galant.'

Rome was the fount of all Clerk's interests, existing and future. There he had built on past knowledge and had developed tastes that would endure for the rest of his life, and in which he would encourage younger generations. 'Music and antiquities' were, he said, his two great diversions during the eighteen months he spent in the city – a long time for any Grand Tourist to devote to a cultural pilgrimage there, then or in later, classic age of the Tour. As a pupil of Arcangelo Corelli in violin (Corelli's only known Scottish pupil) and Bernardo Pasquini at the organ, Clerk was in his element with Cardinal Ottoboni at Palazzo della Cancellaria or at Frascati: he composed for and played with the cardinal's private orchestra, and one of his cantatas of this time, 'Odo di mesto intorno', is now recognized as one of the Scottish musical triumphs of the age. With Corelli he could indulge his artistic interests, too, for Corelli was a great picture collector, and was painted by Hugh Howard, the gentleman amateur and connoisseur who became one of Clerk's closest Roman friends. The foundations of Clerk's collection of antiquities were laid in Rome, that collection later to be praised as the most important in private hands in North Britain when it had been greatly enhanced by Clerk's acquisitions from the sites of Roman Scotland. In the 1720s, with this collection in mind and also Sir John's role as a Maecenas of Scotland in view, the antiquary William Stukeley, who must have envied Clerk his first-hand knowledge of Italy, would laud him as 'a Light for the Muses' in the northern kingdom, the like of which had not been seen since 'the glittering arms of the Romans left it.' Clerk's own paradoxical retrospective assessment of his cultural standing at the time of his return from the Grand Tour was that 'I understood pictures better than became my purse, and as to music I performed rather

The manuscript score of Clerk's cantata 'Odo di mesto intorno', *1698.*

(Clerk of Penicuik Muniments, National Archives of Scotland).

better than became a gentleman.' The dank mists of Scotland had already closed in upon him, shrouding the golden morning glow of youthful promise that had been left behind in Italy.

In 1755 a young man of Clerk's acquaintance wrote of Rome as his 'Holy See of Pleasurable Antiquity'. This young Grand Tourist bought antiquities there, which he thought he might take back to sell to one who had seen the city over half a century before and who would have concurred in that description of its magic as 'the most glorious place in the universal world'. But Clerk was to die that year. That young man was Robert Adam. His ecstatic praise of Rome, conveyed in now celebrated letters preserved among the Clerk papers, captures perfectly Sir John's opinion in his own youth. The letters that Adam wrote, which give such a remarkable and unrivalled picture of what

Rome meant to him and to the generation that had formed his world and shaped his taste, are themselves fortunate survivors of the Penicuik fire. Adam heard from his brother James in Edinburgh of Clerk's death in October 1755, and the young architect and antiquary who now called himself 'Bob the Roman' wrote home thus: 'Baron Clerk, James tells me, is even defunked at last, and the whole town in mourning for his old body.' Adam wondered whether he should lay aside his blue and silver suit and 'lament over the old antiquarian in sack cloth and ashes'. Insouciantly Adam mused: 'It is a pity the bod defunked before he saw some of my antique collection of curiosities. I am sure it would have revived the soul of him for half a dozen years longer.'

A Note on Sources

An essay of this kind, which is a somewhat expanded version of the paper given at the Europa Nostra conference in Edinburgh on 17 September 2007, does not merit the level of provision of notes and references that would be supplied as a matter of course for an article in a learned journal. I offer below, therefore, a note on the sources in general which have informed my work on both the spoken and written version of the paper.

In his own autobiographical writings, published in 1892 as *Memoirs of the Life of Sir John Clerk of Penicuik, Baronet, extracted by himself from his own journals*, Clerk provided an account of his Grand Tour which must have been founded upon his very much more extensive account in the now-lost travel journal. In this excellent edition of Clerk's memoirs John M. Gray was able to draw upon the then-extant travel journal and to include a few extracts from it. These quotations serve mostly to frustrate the modern scholar by pointing up the great loss that the destruction constitutes. The Gray notebooks in the Scottish National Portrait Gallery, especially no 10 in the series, preserve transcripts of other extracts from the contemporary travel journal.

Many of my quotations are taken from letters of John Clerk, his father, the first

Dr Iain Gordon Brown

A Fellow of the Society of Antiquaries of London and the Royal Society of Edinburgh, he is Principal Curator of Manuscripts in the National Library of Scotland. His academic work has concentrated on three areas: British antiquarianism and taste, the art and architecture of the 18th century, and the literature and culture of the age of Walter Scott.

baronet, and many of the younger man's European friends and contemporaries. These correspondences are to be found in the Clerk of Penicuik Muniments deposited in the National Archives of Scotland (GD18). Bundles 5194, 5197, 5202 and 5207 are especially important, and I have drawn upon the letters therein freely and frequently. GD18/ 2095 consists of Clerk's two contemporary dissertations 'On the German Ceremonies' and 'On the Italian Ceremonies'. I have discussed Clerk's Grand Tour at length and in great detail (especially in the annotation) in Chapter 3 of my doctoral thesis, 'Sir John Clerk of Penicuik (1676-1755): Aspects of a Virtuoso Life' (University of Cambridge 1980). See also Iain Gordon Brown 'On Classic Ground: Records of the Grand Tour', *Scottish Archives*, 2 (1996), pp. 1-12. My *The Hobby-Horsical Antiquary* (Edinburgh 1980) deals with Clerk's Grand Tour-inspired antiquarianism in its Scottish context. My review article 'Eighteenth-Century British Antiquaries and Grand Tourists', *Scottish Archives*, 11 (2005), 129-41, surveys recent literature on these topics.

On the Clerk family as cultural leaders over two centuries and through five generations see Iain Gordon Brown, *The Clerks of Penicuik: Portraits of Taste and Talent* (Edinburgh 1987); my entries in *The Dictionary of Art* (London 1996), vol. 7; and (for the eighteenth-century Grand Tourists of the family, but excluding the second baronet as his tour antedated the year 1700) in *A Dictionary of British and Irish Travellers in Italy, 1700-1800*, edited by John Ingamells (New Haven and London 1997). The Clerk collection is dealt with in Iain Gordon Brown, '"I Understood Pictures Better than Became My Purse": The Clerks of Penicuik and Eldin as Collectors and Connoisseurs', *Journal of the Scottish Society for Art History*, 8 (2003), pp. 27-36.

The scores of Clerk's music written while in Holland and Italy are now available in a scholarly edition by Kenneth Elliott, *Five Cantatas by Sir John Clerk of Penicuik* (Glasgow 2005), which includes excellent historical and critical commentaries.

John Fleming's invaluable *Robert Adam and his Circle in Edinburgh and Rome* (London 1962) was the first work to exploit fully the potential of the Clerk Muniments as a source of exceptional value for Grand Tour studies, using as it did the hundreds of letters of Robert and James Adam which, due to family vicissitudes, came to rest at Penicuik. I owe to this fine book, along with Basil Skinner's slighter but excellent *Scots in Italy in the Eighteenth Century* (Edinburgh 1966), my own initial interest in both Sir John Clerk and the more general subjects of the Grand Tour and the British in Italy.

Pompeo Batoni
(1708-1787)
Alexander Gordon,
4th Duke of Gordon
(1743–1827) *1764*

(National Gallery of
Scotland)

Milordi, Artists and Antiquarians

Portraiture of the Grand Tour

Nicola Kalinsky

My aim is to present a general overview of the portraits depicting those Britons who made the Grand Tour in the eighteenth century and to place these portraits within the wider context. I also want to consider whether such portraits can be assessed as a specific genre defined by its own traditions and conventions. Finally, I want to ask the question: what role do these portraits have today in our perception of the Grand Tour and its participants?

I am aiming for broad coverage not depth, and I am largely offering a synopsis of, and cherry picking from, material which is well known in the field and which is fairly accessible in the many books, articles, exhibition catalogues and essays written and published over the last fifty years.

The late Sir Brinsley Ford remains a supremely knowledgeable yet benign presence, presiding over anything to do with the Grand Tour and, to those of you who are new to the subject, I would recommend his essays published over the years in *The Burlington Magazine* and *Apollo* as being as fresh and informative today as when they were written; they still provide the basis for much of what is being published now. The other essential is *A Dictionary of British and Irish Travellers to Italy* 1701 - 1800 published by the Paul Mellon

Centre for Studies in British Art in 1997 and edited and compiled initially by Dr Kim Sloan and subsequently by Dr John Ingamells (cited as Ingamells). This is the ultimate "desert island" book for anyone who loves the characters of the Grand Tour; readable, amusing and informative, it is based largely on the lifetime's worth of research, notes and friendly academic exchanges contained in the Brinsley Ford Archive. I know that our audience today includes people expert in other areas, and for whom this may be an introduction. Hopefully, for these participants, this will be analogous to a new journey, and will convey some of the excitement and cultural enrichment of the Grand Tour itself.

What follows falls into three parts. Firstly, I will examine the antecedents and early history of the classic Grand Tour portrait; secondly, I want to sketch in a context for Grand Tour portraiture of the mid and later eighteenth century, focussing particularly on Rome, and thirdly, I will look at a range of portraits of Grand Tourists from this period and place.

Grand Tour Portraiture to 1750

The history of Grand Tour portraiture naturally enough shares its trajectory with the Grand Tour itself, the journey and those who undertook it provide these portraits with their specific types of sitters, their geographical locations, and therefore their artists, and the commercial and social nexus within which these objects were commissioned and made.

When we think of a typical Grand Tour portrait we probably have in mind something like the portrait of Sir Edward Dering by Pompeo Batoni, a work in a private collection (see *Pompeo Batoni Complete Catalogue*, Anthony M Clark, London, 1985, no 216, pl.7, cited subsequently as Clark) on long-term loan to the Art Institute of Chicago. Painted in Rome in 1758/59, this portrait presents a handsome young man of wealth, apparently possessed of aesthetic good taste and intellectual discernment. Dering is dressed in sumptuous fur-trimmed velvet and satin and regards the viewer thoughtfully, looking up from his open book, as if to converse with us on the merits of the antique cameo in his right hand. A bust version of the Apollo Belvedere and a faithful Italian greyhound convey their approval in their different and appropriate ways. Portraits such as this by Batoni were, in their own time, the iconic images of the Grand Tourists and, displayed in their intended original context of the ancestral home, framed how these young men were perceived by fellow members of the British ruling classes. Batoni, as we shall see, is the classic portrait painter of the Grand Tour, in terms of both quality and quantity. But, as has often been pointed out, just as the Grand Tour did not appear fully formed from nowhere in the mid-eighteenth century, so the Grand Tour portrait has its own precedents and precursors, fascinating for both their similarities and differences to what was to come.

There is a considerable body of evidence tracing the evolution of the British Grand Tour back to the last quarter of the sixteenth century, when continental travel for educational and cultural purposes, as distinct from religious, mercantile or diplomatic reasons, began to be considered highly desirable for young men destined to play an active role in public life as adults. There are no paintings extant of these Elizabethan pioneers that I know of, but, by the seventeenth century, many of the traditions that we associate with the classic Grand Tour began to develop, such as, for example, the bringing home of souvenirs - books, prints, paintings, antiquities and curios. Sir Brinsley Ford mentioned a handful of portraits pre 1700 but made the vital point that these were exceptions, both in terms of the oeuvre of the particular artist and the experience of the traveller. The earliest image known and published is a work of 1647 by Matteo Bolognini of three English gentlemen perusing a map of Italy (Canterbury Dean and Chapter, see *Grand Tour, The Lure of Italy in the C18th*, Tate, London, 1996, no. 49, cited subsequently as Grand Tour). Painted in Siena, it shows an older man, John Bargrave, in the middle, with his nephew, John Raymond, to his right, and another travelling companion. Bargrave, an Anglican clergyman, is an early example of a travelling tutor, of which more later, and the reasons for his exile from England - expulsion on religious/political grounds - were not unusual. However, whilst the circumstances and characters of this painting resonate strongly with the later period, as an image it is very unlike the elegant Batoni, being more an earnest, documentary sort of object.

Moving into the early 1700s, the trickle of British travellers to continental Europe becomes more insistent, partly for reasons of periodic or permanent exile, but mainly due to a growing sense amongst Britain's elite of a need and a right to participate in a civilisation which they were increasingly dominating in spheres military and economic. We will now find more and more examples of portraits of Britons undertaken during and recording their Grand Tour, works which begin to suggest the emergence of a visual tradition, albeit one based heavily on the standard flourishes of late Italian Baroque portraiture.

First, an example by Andrea Procaccini of James, Lord Johnstone, later 2nd Marquess of Annandale, an early Scottish Grand Tourist. The portrait is listed in family inventories as having been commissioned in Italy in 1718. The architectural setting and enveloping draperies are all typically Baroque, but the sitter draws particular attention to his status as a connoisseur of the cultural bounty of the Grand Tour, holding a small bronze of Minerva in his right hand. Coins lie on his papers beside a miniature portrait and an antique fragmented torso occupies the bottom corner of the canvas. His costume is also possibly significant, with stockings and short boots or buskins giving him a vaguely Roman military appearance, from the thighs down at least. Other examples include one by Francesco Trevisani, a Venetian who worked in Rome, of Thomas Coke, later the 1st Earl of Leicester, painted in 1717 (Holkham Hall, Norfolk), and of Sir Edward Gascoigne, painted in 1725 (Temple Newsam, Leeds). The interior setting of Coke's portrait is flamboyantly Baroque, with its swagged curtain and over-animated chair. In the architectural niches we see versions, possibly plasters, of the Venus de Medici and Farnese Hercules. The adoring dog looking up to its master is a motif which we will encounter frequently in Grand Tour portraits. Coke, who embarked on his Grand Tour at the age of 15, accompanied by his tutor, sat for at least two other portraits, including a pastel in Venice by Rosalba Carriera. Gascoigne was a Yorkshire Catholic who travelled with his physician and a French tutor. Here, he pauses from reading his copy of Horace, to glance at the viewer and gesture through the open window to the ruins of the Colosseum.

The very artists to whom one might sit in Rome at this time were those patronised by the exiled Stuarts, resident in the city since 1719. Antonio David, another painter popular with the Jacobite Court, produced several Grand Tour portraits of Britons from the mid 1730s, such as William Perry, 1736 (location unknown), and George Lewis Coke, 1735 (private collection). Once again, the generalised Baroque setting is given more specific connotations, this time through the inclusion of the open view to a

Andrea Procaccini (1671-1734)
James, Lord Johnstone, later 2nd Marquess of Annandale, *(1688-1721) 1718*

(Hopetoun House Preservation Trust)
Photo Ian Boyter

quintessential Roman view of the Colosseum. Coke further emphasises his cultural engagement by gesturing towards the globe on the table. Ten years on, in Andrea Casali's portrait of Charles Frederick (Ashmolean, Oxford), we have the typical grand setting of columns, curtains and ornate furniture, opening onto a view of the Pantheon.

These pre 1750 examples of Grand Tour portraiture lead me to make two observations: all the portraits are by Italians – or, in the case of Antonio David, Swiss Italian – and all were painted in Rome. Although there are quite a few examples of resident or travelling British artists in Italy producing portraits during this period – for example the Aberdonian John Alexander painted Thomas Coke in Rome in 1714 – there was not as yet the large community of British and other Northern European artists in Italy that emerged in the second half of the century. Secondly, just as the Grand Tour began to focus on Italy at this time, so its portraiture becomes ever more closely associated with Italy and, above all, with Rome. There are examples of British travellers having their portraits made in the other countries typically visited during the Grand Tour – France, Germany, Austria and the Low Countries, but I would hazard a guess that the images will be less concerned with documenting the actual location of the sitting as evidence of travel and its desired effects. This supposition I would not apply to portraits painted elsewhere in Italy, of which there were many, from 1700 onwards, especially from Venice and Naples, but concentrating on Rome, as I will do now, is logical, as the overwhelming majority of Grand Tour portraits were undertaken in the Eternal City.

As we now move on to the second part of this talk, I want to summarise an embryo aesthetic which these portraits begin to embody: the sitter, in a grand setting – so far all interiors – is usually shown in a way which indicates his status as one imbibing the cultural knowledge which was the central goal of the Grand Tour. Reading or writing, or pausing from these activities, he may have antique pieces about him and his room may look out to a very obvious Roman building, usually a ruin from the period of Rome's classical greatness rather than a Renaissance or Baroque edifice.

Let's return now to our Batoni portrait of Dering and use it to begin to sketch in the context which existed beyond the canvas and which meshed the sitter into a particular social and practical nexus of human relationships, of

Pier Leone Ghezzi (1674-1755)
Dr James Hay (d. 1746) as Bear-Leader *c. 1725*
Pen and brown ink

(Trustees of the British Museum)

which a portrait was just one possible outcome. Dering made his Grand Tour between 1758 and 59. On his return home, he visited Horace Walpole and got drunk. Walpole, writing to his friend, Horace Mann, the British representative in Florence who acted as a first point of contact for most British visitors to Italy, described Dering as a 'foolish Kentish knight' and ribbed his friend for having been too open with their correspondence to visiting young Britons. ' For mercy's sake, take care how you communicate my letter to such cubs – I will send you no more invasions, if you read them to bears and to bear-leaders' (Clark, p.275).

Walpole's comments conjure up a less than ideal vision of the supposedly ardent student of culture, a view of the traveller more like that seen in the caricature drawn by Pier Leone Ghezzi. This shows the famous travelling tutor Dr James Hay with a pupil in tow (Trustees of the British Museum, London, see Grand Tour, no 54). The young men on the Grand Tour – and the majority were young, the average age of Batoni's sitters being 22 – were usually accompanied, at the very least, by a tutor, usually an older, trusted, man, who supervised the experience and prevented the worst excesses, financial or personal. This became a recognised form of employment for educated professionals – often doctors or university professors – who would not necessarily have had the independent means to fund a long continental journey. It was also, on occasion, a handy occupation for Britons in political and religious exile. Hay, a Jacobite Scot, supervised the tours of at least eight young Britons between 1704 and 1734, and this caricature was drawn around the time he was taking William Robinson, son of Sir Tancred Robinson, through Italy in the early 1720s. Hay's image was, presumably, a recognisable caricature to contemporaries, but the unidentified young man is shown as a ludicrous small bear cub, pulled along by his cuff, implying the green foolishness of many of these youths.

We see a more official version of this tutor/pupil relationship in Gavin Hamilton's portrait of Douglas Hamilton, 8th Duke of Hamilton, with his travelling companion, Dr John Moore and Moore's young son, painted between 1775 and 1777 (Scottish National Portrait Gallery, Edinburgh). As the tutor was not usually a specialist in what needed to be seen, ancient or modern, it was normal practice in Rome and in some of the other centres of the Grand Tour, notably Naples, to employ the services of a resident antiquarian or guide to organise and lead the sight-seeing and visits. In Moore's later published account of his European travels with the duke, he recalled: 'What is called a regular course with an Antiquarian, generally takes up about six weeks; employing three hours a day, you may, in that time, visit all the churches, palaces, villas and ruins, worth seeing, in or near Rome'. (A View of Society and Manners in Italy John Moore, London, 1787, Letter XLV).

Prior to about 1750 the role of the antiquarian or cicerone, as they

Gavin Hamilton (1723-1795)
Douglas Hamilton, 8th Duke of Hamilton *(1756-1799),* with Dr John Moore, *(1729-1802)* his tutor and Ensign John Moore *(1761-1809)* 1775-7

(Scottish National Portrait Gallery)

were also known, had usually been filled by Italians, but, from the 1740s, this niche employment attracted a number of failed British artists and architects, who became pivotal figures within the Grand Tour experience. James Russel was one of the first, working as guide to tourists in Rome from around 1740 until his death in 1763 – there is a painting of Irish and English gentleman on the Tour which has been attributed to Russel (Yale Center for British Art, Paul Mellon Collection, see Grand Tour, no 43). After Russel, two figures dominated until well into the 1790s – Thomas Jenkins and the Scot, James Byres. It was Byres who guided the Duke of Hamilton and John Moore on their 'regular course' in the winter of 1775/76. Other antiquarians who operated in Rome included Colin Morison, a Scottish artist who took up the profession after damaging his eyesight, and the more amateurish Abbé Peter Grant, a sociable Jesuit Priest.

The antiquarians, in daily contact with visitors, had privileged access to young men who were often seriously rich (the Duke of Hamilton's travel allowance was £1200 per annum at a time when a skilled printer might earn £50 per annum). These wealthy boys were beyond immediate parental control, supervised by their social inferiors, and were, as part of the Grand Tour, expected to make acquisitions. The provision of what might call connected services – introductions to artists, acting as bankers, dealing in old masters and antiquities, negotiating export licences and organising shipping arrangements – further cemented the lucrative relationship between antiquarians and Grand Tourists and could provide a good living. Jenkins's country retreat in Castel Gandolfo was described as 'a sort of trap' for rich young Englishmen 'prepared to spend large sums on antiquities' and Dr John Moore, writing to the Duke of Hamilton's mother from Rome, lamented the fact that the young man was beginning to show 'a great inclination to make purchases. This desire is always mightily encouraged by a set of designing People in Italy' (Intimate Society Letters of the C18th ed. Duke of Argyll, Vol. II, 24 May 1776). Portraiture, along with the purchase of Roman, Venetian and Neapolitan vedute and capriccii, and the more occasional bold commissioning of a history painting, takes its place within the overall spending patterns of the Grand Tour. But, of all that one might go home with, apart from the pox, a portrait was probably the most expected and most economical

Pompeo Batoni (1708-1787)
John, Lord Brudenell, later Marquis of Monthermer
(1735-1770), 1758
(Boughton House)

(by permission of the Duke of Buccleuch and Queensberry)

souvenir. Even those many Grand Tourists who never entered the spirit of accumulating a great collection of old masters or marbles would feel it incumbent to take home a portrait to document their experience, much to the disgust of Dr John Moore, who wondered why it should be that 'every periwig-pated fellow, without countenance or character, insist[s] on seeing his chubby cheeks on canvas?' (Moore, op. cit, letter L).

The case of John, Lord Brudenell, demonstrates well the fruitful interconnections which existed between milordi, artists and antiquarians. This is Lord Brudenell in a portrait by Pompeo Batoni painted in 1758/59 (Duke of Buccleuch and Queensberry, Boughton House, Northants, Clark, no 202, pl.6) Lord Brudenell commenced his Grand Tour at the age of 17 with his tutor, Henry Lyte. After a couple of years in France, they arrived in Italy in 1754, where they spent the next six years. Lord Brudenell was a considerable collector, with Jenkins acting as his agent in Rome. He is reckoned to have spent around £2,000 on paintings and, in one period of just 9 months, 4 export licenses were granted to him, mainly for antique marbles. In Naples he commissioned views from Antonio Joli and in Venice, from Guardi. In Rome he sat to Batoni and to the German artist resident in Rome, Anton Raphael Mengs, both of whom could have been recommended by Jenkins, although, by this date, it was a commonplace that Batoni was the best and his studio and exhibition rooms were themselves part of the tourist itinerary. Batoni and Mengs also benefited from the recommendations of Cardinal Albani who advised and gave practical help to British travellers in Rome. Batoni's work, and his trajectory from being, in the 1730s and 40s, Rome's leading history and religious painter, to becoming a portraitist dominated by a British clientele, has been well documented. We know that Brudenell was just one of around 150 Britons who sat to Batoni and the overwhelming number of his clients - around 79% - were British. During his long career, Batoni only painted the portraits of about 20 Italians.

Turning again to Brudenell, and to this beautiful portrait, I want to emphasise that, although British visitors constantly complained about the expense of going to Batoni, what they got - a painting by the man considered to be the best artist in Italy - was a great bargain. In the 1750s he charged the equivalent of £15 for a half-length, when Sir Joshua Reynolds or Thomas Hudson in London were charging £24, and, in the 1760s, when the great, complex full-lengths come on stream, Batoni was charging £25 to Reynolds's £150. Another comparison to demonstrate the excellent value - the Duke of Rutland spent £2,000 on Poussin's Seven Sacraments and Sir William Hamilton paid £1000 for the Portland Vase.

Mengs was the only real rival in terms of status to Batoni, but Mengs was absent from Rome for exactly that part of the 1750s when the portrait business really took off and, contrary to Batoni, he was as interested in expanding his career as a history painter just at the point when Batoni seems to take the opposite decision. Looking at Mengs's portrait of Brudenell (Duke of Buccleuch and Queensberry, Boughton House, Northants), it is actually the more obvious in its presentation of the signs or emblems of the Grand Tour experience. In comparison, the Batoni seems more individualised in its reaction to the sitter (Brudenell is holding a manuscript score of Corelli's Opus 5). Batoni can demonstrate a very sensitive response to an individual sitter if and when a sitter is a person of inherent interest, as for example, in the portrait of James Bruce of Kinnaird, 1762 (Scottish National Portrait Gallery, Edinburgh, Clark no.258), but, on the whole, Batoni seems to have been spurred on by competition with Mengs's grander manner, and to have adopted a more generalised and ambitious approach.

The portraits which best demonstrate this new ambition are ones such as that of Sir Wyndham Knatchbull Wyndam, painted in 1758- 59 (Private Collection, Clark no. 218 pl. 19). The twenty-two year old, dressed in Van Dyck masquerade costume, is placed in a setting of some grandeur - swags, tassel, columns, marble floor. In a dramatic pose adapted from the Apollo Belvedere, Wyndam gestures to the open view out to the Temple of the Sybil (Vesta) at Tivoli. A bust version of the Minerva Giustiniani sits in the shadows, an Italian greyhound leaps up adoringly. The quotation of the pose of probably the most iconic Antique statue in Rome is interesting as it seems to me, in comparison with the use made of the Apollo by Reynolds and Ramsay, quite unforced - Wyndham's pose is so self-consciously theatrical that it seems, paradoxically, entirely natural.

Juxtaposing Batoni's 1774 portrait of Thomas William Coke (Holkham Hall, Norfolk, Clark No 377, Pl 340) to Van Dyck's 1634 portrait of the Earl of Warwick (Metropolitan Museum, New York) demonstrates one source of inspiration for Batoni's ability to suggest a seamless union between patrician authority and easy elegance. It has been suggested that Batoni was well aware of Van Dyck, and learnt from the Fleming's subtle use of pose to suggest restrained yet authoritative characterisation. Batoni would also have been well aware of how this artist had defined a look and almost a self-definition for the British aristocracy.

Pompeo Batoni
James Bruce of Kinnaird *(1730-1794) 1762*

(Scottish National Portrait Gallery)

By way of an anecdote, Coke is in elaborate masquerade dress, and it was assumed at the time when the portrait was painted that this was the actual costume Coke had worn at a ball given in Rome in 1773 when he danced with the Countess of Albany, the wife of Prince Charles Edward Stuart. It was she, apparently, who commissioned this painting from Batoni, and the features of the statue of the Vatican Cleopatra (now known as Ariadne) were said to resemble her. Walpole wrote ' The young Mr Coke is returned from his travels in love with the Pretender's Queen, who has permitted him to have her picture' (Clark, p.333).

Another British traveller who had a close encounter with the charming but unhappily married Countess of Albany was the young Duke of Hamilton, whom we have already seen in the portrait by Gavin Hamilton. The duke was also painted by Batoni, fitting in the two or three sittings needed during a brief stopover in Rome on the return leg of his travels through Italy. Rather more conventional than the Hamilton portrait (see Clark, no 388, pl.352), Batoni deploys what, by the 1770s, is his repertoire of 'Grand Tour' elements - the statue of Roma above the relief of the Weeping Dacia, the Temple of Vesta at Tivoli, and an antique fragment with a headless Griffin, this latter most probably a studio prop. Dr Moore, writing to the duchess, noted how 'the Face only was finished when we left Rome'. This was the usual practice, as Batoni only required his client's presence for capturing the facial features; pose, setting and accoutrements were worked up subsequently. Batoni was immensely familiar with the antiquities of Rome, having drawn them repeatedly during his early years in the city. In his portraits he draws on this knowledge but he usually utilises a relatively small number of well-known antique pieces or adaptations from them, and the most obvious distant views to the Temple of the Vesta or the Colosseum, which he uses repeatedly. Quite what input his clients had in the choice of antique statue, we don't know, but it seems likely that most sitters would have wanted the obvious pieces listed in their guide-books, unless they had a special reason for a particular statue, as in the example of Coke and Cleopatra. Batoni, to my knowledge, never includes in the background a painted reference to a canonical painting of the Renaissance or the Baroque. This could be partly explained by the growing fashion for neo-classicism and acquiring marbles, but, that said, paintings from

Nathaniel Dance (1735-1811)
James Grant of Grant, *(1738-1811)* John Mytton, *(1737-1783)* Thomas Robinson *(1738-1786)* and Thomas Wynn, *(1736-1807)* in front of the Colosseum in Rome
c. 1760

(Yale Centre for British Art, Paul Mellon Collection)

the more recent past were still as eagerly sought after by our Grand Tourists.

For the poses of his sitters, Batoni drew on a stock of positions and gestures which he re-used, although always with minor adaptations. It has been convincingly suggested that Batoni was not, in this, uninfluenced by British portraiture of the 1740s and 50s, in particular the easy poses of conversation pieces - for example, the casually crossed legs and elbow on plinth stance. These English works, by artists like Francis Hayman and Thomas Gainsborough, also provided examples of relaxed outdoor settings, often with a view to a recognisable building.

One direct source of this influence was the younger English artist Nathaniel Dance, who was resident in Rome from 1754 to 1765 and who had trained in London with Francis Hayman before coming to Italy. Dance became closely connected with Batoni, at one point even sharing a business card. Dance was in Rome primarily to acquire the knowledge and contacts to become a history painter and to make himself a more serious artist than Hayman, who had never visited Rome, and who was ridiculed by the younger generation for his mannerisms and poor colouring. But Dance, who also had considerable success in obtaining commissions for portraits of Grand Tourists, wrote to his father from Rome, conceding that Hayman had 'great facility of invention' (Nathaniel Dance, GLC, Iveagh Bequest, London, 1977).

In a painting of 1760 by Dance we see four British travellers of means - from left to right - the Scot, James Grant of Grant, Thomas Wynn, later Baron Newborough, Thomas Robinson and John Mytton (Yale Center for British Art, Paul Mellon Collection, see Grand Tour, no 14). Before we consider the image, just a few points about the sitters - Grant was shown around Rome by Abbé Peter Grant and commissioned several paintings besides his portrait, including landscapes by John Plimmer and historical pieces with classical subject matter from Colin Morison, Nathaniel Dance and Gavin Hamilton. Hamilton's great history painting for Grant, Achilles mourning Patroclus, now belongs to the National Gallery of Scotland. Robinson was also painted by Mengs.

In the group portrait at Yale, one of the four versions Dance painted for each of the sitters, we see the now familiar motifs of Grand Tour portraiture - a view of the Colosseum and a prominent piece of antique sculpture, in this case an imaginary urn with figures based on the well-known relief then called the Borghese Dancers (now in the reserve collection of Louvre). These classical elements are combined with the sitters' relaxed and fashionable body language – for example, the casual arrangement of the seated Mr Robinson, as he looks up from a plan of the Temple of Jupiter Stator to Mytton, who is leaning with crossed legs against the plinth. All this is very reminiscent of poor despised Hayman, who had even included a version of an urn with classical dancers in a conversation piece of circa 1750/52 (compare to Mr and Mrs Tyers, Yale Center for British Art, Paul Mellon Collection).

Another example by Dance at Hopetoun is of Charles, Lord Hope and the Honourable James Hope, with their tutor William Rouet, a professor of Oriental Languages at the University of Glasgow (Private Collection). Painted in 1763-64, Dance includes an antique urn, a bust and a distant view, not to a ruin of classical Rome, but to St Peters. Dance also painted full-lengths of the two Hope brothers individually (James Hope – the healthy one – was painted with Tivoli in the background). Conversely, although Batoni was influenced by Dance, he never painted conversation pieces of small full-length figures in the English manner, but strictly applied their lessons to the traditional scale of full and half length portraiture.

We can equally see the influence of this English manner in a work by Anton von Maron, an Austrian artist who had trained, alongside Byres, with Mengs in Rome. He was a great favourite of both Byres and Jenkins, who frequently recommended him to British travellers. A typical example is Maron's full-size full-length of Robert Grimston of Neswick Hall (Private Collection), who was in Italy in 1767 - 68. Grimston, who was something of a connoisseur, exporting 23 paintings from Rome, reckoned Maron to be 'the best painter' (Ingamells, p 435).

If the last two works begin to seem a little formulaic, which is a criticism some Grand Tour portraiture merits, we should return to Batoni to look briefly at two of his most flamboyant and successful portraits of Scots - that of the two Gordons, uncle and nephew. Alexander Gordon, 4th Duke of Gordon (National Gallery of Scotland, Edinburgh, Clark no 258), painted by Batoni in 1764, was notorious for dozing off in his carriage whilst the great historian and neo-classical theorist Winckelmann discoursed on the ancient sights of Rome.

The duke preferred hunting. The portrait of his uncle, Colonel William Gordon, of 1766 (Fyvie Castle, Aberdeenshire, National Trust for Scotland, Clark no. 298) which has attracted much scholarly interest, not least because of Batoni's interpretation of the tartan kilt, draped in the manner of a Roman toga, is justly famous. James Boswell chummed up with Colonel Gordon in Rome; together they visited St Peters with Abbé Grant on Maundy Thursday, 1765, and, a couple of weeks later, Boswell saw Batoni painting the drapery of Gordon's portrait, and thought this worth recording. Boswell, who is like no one else, did not choose Batoni or Mengs or Maron for his own Grand Tour portrait, but sat to a fellow Scot, George Willison in 1765 (Scottish National Portrait Gallery, Edinburgh) for what is an entirely atypical example of the genre.

To conclude and return to the typical Grand Tour portrait, what role should these images play in our perception of the Grand Tour today, when we are as likely to meet them in the public museum as the private house, and the 'we' who are entitled to look on them have expanded democratically beyond the wildest imaginings of the sitters?

Unquestionably, these portraits by Batoni, Mengs, Maron or Dance and others must be classed among the official images of the Grand Tour, recording and presenting the young traveller in the process of successfully absorbing the lessons of civilisation. Before young Grimston travelled to the Continent, he told his parents that he intended to 'polish myself so far that when I come home again you shall all wonder and say Is this the clownish school Boy, whom I knew two years ago' (Ingamells, p.435). On returning from the Grand Tour, we are to assume that our cubs will be men, and men of taste, and thus qualified to lead this civilisation of which they were the fortunate inheritors.

Now, obviously, as with all such portraits of asserted status, and with all such high ideals, there will be gaps of varying dimensions between the vision and the reality. We could have looked at more caricatures of the Grand Tour, which poke fun at all the characters, although they never question the underlying assumptions of the Grand Tour as a cultural enterprise, only the inadequacy of individuals. We could read, alongside the official travel literature and journals, the private correspondence and diaries of travellers, which inevitably give a more nuanced picture of the process (this is the focus of many recent

George Willison (1741-1799)
James Boswell *(1740-1795) 1765*

(Scottish National Portrait Gallery)

Nicola Kalinsky

Chief Curator and Deputy Director of the Scottish National Portrait Gallery, having previously been Curator of the college art collections of University College London and Keeper of Dulwich Picture Gallery. Has taught art history for the Open University, Ealing College and Birkbeck College, as well as curating many exhibitions, both here and abroad.

publications on the Grand Tour). Even the willing Grimston, on his return, admitted that 'not even two years & a half that I have been rolling about, can give me a sufficient Impudence to fancy that I am wise or know more than all the world besides myself, which a young man generally does, after coming home from abroad' (Ingamells, p 435).

Yet, even bearing this in mind, it can still be accepted that the cultural aims of the Grand Tour existed as an entirely real aspiration for many, even the majority, of visitors to Italy. It is remarkable that so many of these young men really developed a sustained interest in the cultural riches around them and their deep engagement is not adequately explained away by their prior education or the impulses of fashion. The comparison, made so often, with today's gap year students can be illuminating rather than trite, but largely for the differences between the two phenomena. Today's girls and boys of relative privilege usually want to travel beyond Europe and to experience the other, the exotic, the non-Western. The goals are no longer cultural acquisition in the traditional, rather literal, sense, but are rather defined by notions of global social contribution - the accumulation of a different kind of virtue. Perhaps this only and inevitably reflects our very different world, as compared to that inhabited by the Grand Tourists, and results from what one might describe as our post-modern awareness of our historical contingency and marginality. Whatever we ascribe these differences to, they might make us appreciate all the more the particular vision of the Grand Tour portraits of the eighteenth century.

Sources and Bibliography

A Dictionary of British and Irish Travellers to Italy 1701 - 1800 John Ingamells, Yale University Press, New Haven and London, 1997

Pompeo Batoni Complete Catalogue Anthony M. Clark ed Edgar Peters Bowron Oxford, 1985

Grand Tour: The Lure of Italy in the Eighteenth Century, ed Andrew Wilton and Ilaria Bignamini, Tate, London, 1996

Designs for interior decoration from The Works in Architecture of Robert and James Adam *(1773-78)*

Opposite:

George Willison (1741-1799), Robert Adam *(1728-92) 1765 pictured holding his study of Diocletion's Palace at Split (1764)*

(by permission of the National Portrait Gallery, London)

Italy and the
Making of Robert Adam

Lester Borley

Robert Adam died at his home at 13 Albemarle Street in London at the beginning of March 1792, and a week later was buried in Westminster Abbey (where his arch-rival Sir William Chambers was to join him four years later). At the funeral, his pall-bearers included the Duke of Buccleuch, the Earl of Coventry and the Earl of Lauderdale, among other prominent clients, and the great pomp of his funeral indicated quite clearly his considerable reputation as the creator of a style which would bear his name for ever.

Robert was born on 3 July 1728 in Kirkcaldy, the second son of William and Mary (née Robertson) Adam. In that same year William Adam moved his family to Edinburgh, where Robert was to be educated at the High School and subsequently studied Classics at the Town's College (now University of Edinburgh) at a time of great political and social disruption caused by the Jacobite Rebellion of 1745/6.

Like his older brother John (born 1721) Robert was to be apprenticed in 1746 to his father in the burgeoning enterprise of architecture, building and related enterprises. It was an opportunity for the brothers, later to be joined by James (born in 1732) to become totally immersed in the business of building and the profession of architecture, in which their father was pre-eminent in Scotland. William's design in 1730 for the House of Dun in Angus commissioned by Lord Erskine, was influenced by the ideas of the Earl of Mar, who had been exiled to France for his part in the failed Jacobite uprising of 1715. The main north front of the house employs a design which was unusual in Scotland for the time, and which showed the growing interest of the family in the architectural styles of other countries.

In 1728 William Adam had been appointed Clerk and Store Keeper of the Works in Scotland and two years later became Master Mason to the Board of Ordnance in Scotland. With his increasing prosperity he was able to acquire the small estate of Blair Cambreth near Kinross, the name of which was changed to Blair Adam, and which is still in the ownership of the family. In due course William bought further land to the north at Dowhill, and on his death in 1748 this was left to Robert, which in due course enabled him, as a landowner in his own right, to stand for Parliament and become MP for Kinross-shire in 1769, at a time when the brothers would be deeply involved in the ill-fated Adelphi scheme.

The principal project on which the Adam family was to establish its reputation was the enhancement of Hopetoun House near Edinburgh, originally designed by Sir William Bruce. When Charles Hope became the first Earl of Hopetoun he was clearly in need of a more splendid "House of State".

William Adam was of course also at this time engaged in lucrative Government contracts, particularly for the Board of Ordnance. After Culloden in 1746, the Government was determined that the Highlands should never again be threatened by the Stuart Pretenders.

Inverness was particularly vulnerable from the sea and it was decided to build a new Fort George on Vauban principles at Ardersier to the east. This project would engage the family for ten years, giving the sons experience of large-scale project management and bringing a substantial income from which Robert Adam was able to undertake his Grand Tour in 1754. His share of the partnership profits amounted to about £5,000 (about £300,000 at 2008 prices) This of course was a wise investment, not only for the social pleasures of the Grand Tour, but also for the new ideas which he would gather, and for the art objects which he was able to acquire for the architectural practice which he was

House of Dun *(1730)*
by William Adam (1698-1748)
Engraving

(National Trust for Scotland)

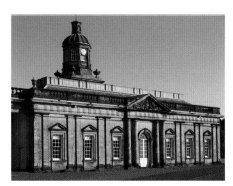

Stable Block, Hopetoun House *(c. 1750)*
by John and Robert Adam

(photo by Lester Borley)

Pier Leone Ghezzi *(1674-1755)*
Charles-Louis Clérisseau
Pen and ink

(the Trustees of the British Museum)

G. B. Piranesi (1720-1778)
Dedication to Robert Adam on Ichnographia
Campi Martii, (1757)

to establish eventually with James in London.

His Grand Tour began in the company of the Hon. Charles Hope who, at the suggestion of his brother the Earl of Hopetoun was off on his own Grand Tour at the age of 43, intending to visit his son William who was already on his Grand Tour at the age of 18. Robert Adam at this time was aged 26, and his letters home show that he and Charles Hope had few interests in common and they were to go their own ways once in Rome.

Robert Adam's Grand Tour followed a well-defined route to Paris, south to Marseilles and then to Genoa and Leghorn to Florence, before arriving at the height of the pre-Lenten carnival season. Horace Mann, who was the British Minister to the Tuscan Court and the host to many travelling milordi, did not immediately take to Robert Adam, but the latter was more fortunate in his chance meeting at the home of Ignazio Hugford with a French architect and draughtsman, Charles Louis Clérisseau, who was on his way home having been expelled from the French Academy in Rome. Robert Adam recognised immediately Clérisseau's talent for drawing and savoir faire, and persuaded him to return to Rome in his employ. This was to be one of the most significant meetings and decisions of Adam's life.

In his letters home he claimed a close friendship with Clérisseau, but one must assume that this was primarily one of convenience as Adam was well aware of the competition that he faced from other aspiring architects such as William Chambers and Robert Mylne, who were in Italy at the time. Robert Adam took his studies seriously and through Clérisseau was able to meet other distinguished artists such as Laurent Pecheux, Anton Raphael Mengs and Pompeo Batoni, but it is undoubtedly because of Clérisseau that Adam became a more proficient draughtsman and dedicated student of classical antiquity.

Adam was also to become friendly with Giovanni Batista Piranesi, a most creative printmaker and antiquarian, whose powerful engravings of the antiquities of Rome were very popular with milordi. Piranesi not only praised Adam's drawings but also suggested dedicating one of his engravings to him. This was to be in the form of an antique inscription on the dedication plate of Piranesi's work Ichnographia Campi Martii (1757). However Piranesi required something in return and Robert Adam records that he planned to purchase 80 or so copies of it, for re-sale in London. Adam's name was also to appear on a memorial in one of the frontispiece plates to Volume II of the *Antichità Romane* (1756) by Piranesi.

Adam would owe his growing ability as a draughtsman to Clérisseau, but it was the imaginative power of Piranesi's engravings, particularly the theatrical *capriccii* that inspired Adam's bravura designs for his wealthier clients in due time.

Adam was always conscious of his reputation relative to other young architects, and saw the need to take on an original project to be noticed. He first thought that he might try to produce an improved version of Desgodetz's *Les Edifices Antiques de Rome*, but although he employed his draughtsmen in the preliminary work, this was soon abandoned. Lisbon had suffered a devastating earthquake in 1755 and Adam even considered that he might suggest a plan for the reconstruction of the city, but that was just a fanciful dream.

He was envious of the growing stature of those who had taken time to study and publish their work on ancient sites.. Robert Wood's *Ruins of Palmyra* (1753), followed by his other work on the *Ruins of Balbec* (1757) had made his reputation.. Stuart and Revett had recently surveyed and drawn the *Antiquities of Athens* (to be published in 1762), and Adam realised that he needed to find something suitably challenging. He had heard of the ruins of the palace of Domitian (sic) at Spalatro in Dalmatia (now Split in Croatia). They were in fact the ruins of the palace of the Emperor Diocletian, and he determined to record them with his team of draughtsmen following the visit to Venice which would mark the last stage of his Grand Tour.

By late 1756, Adam was aware that he would be close to exhausting the money that he had amassed for his Grand Tour. His draughtsmen, Dewez and Brunias, were employed to record important secular buildings, such as Hadrian's Villa and the Baths of Diocletian and Caracalla. These were to provide him not only with a detailed study of the great architecture of Imperial Rome, but also with a unique stock of classical motifs to inspire his future designs.

He prepared for his return to England after a final visit to Venice. He still needed to undertake the excursion to Dalmatia to study and draw the ruins of Diocletian's Palace, whose publication he felt sure would place him in the same league as Wood, Stuart and Revett.

The view towards the Iron Gate from the later market place
(Drawing by John Knight 1987)

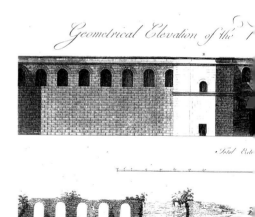

The drawings of the east wall of the Palace as found Adam and his conjectural reconstruction. (1757)

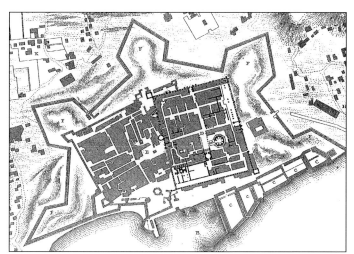

Spalatro: *Robert Adam's plan of the Palace, later Venetian development and baroque fortifications (1757, published 1764)*

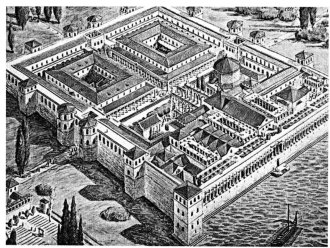

Conjectural drawing by Hebrand (1912) showing not only the Imperial Palace but also the additional domestic and defence structures

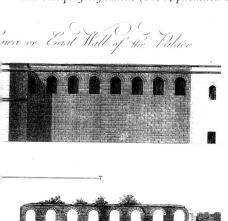

(Lester Borley collection)

Diocletian was born in humble circumstances in Dalmatia in 245AD. He prospered and was proclaimed Emperor by the army in 284AD, and reigned within a tetrarchy which he formed with three other rulers, each of whom was responsible for a different part of the Empire. He spent most of his time on the Danube or in the east of the Empire, and in fact he only visited Rome on one occasion in 303AD, retiring to his boyhood home in 305AD where he died in his palace in 313AD.

The Imperial Palace stood about five kilometres south of the important Roman seaport of Salona, and in time the palace became a refuge for the inhabitants of Salona when overrun by Slavic tribes on the collapse of the Roman Empire. 1400 years later Diocletian's Palace had become obscured by the layers of medieval, Venetian and baroque building of Spalatro, and Adam and Clérisseau were faced with a complex site to record in the five weeks allowed them by the Venetian Republic. Adam knew Diocletian's Palace to be one of the key buildings of late antique architecture, a synthesis of imperial palace and a castrum built by oriental masters from Asia Minor and Syria, which had been studied in 1730 by the Austrian court architect, Fischer von Erlach.

The palace building is of a quadrangular form divided by two main streets

95

leading to four different gates (gold, silver, bronze and iron). The main (golden) gate did not, as one might expect, face the sea but looked to the north towards Salona. This golden gate was in a reasonable state of repair and its central doorway arch is now considered by Alistair Rowan to be the inspiration for the fanlight which would become a key element of 18th century entrance design.

Guests of the Emperor approaching the palace from the golden gate would have followed the cardo towards the peristyle (forecourt), ascending by a flight of steps through the porticus, which in turn led into a circular vestibule, into an atrium (great hall), and subsequently into the cryptoporticus (open gallery) from which there was access to other imperial apartments. It was the arrangement of such spaces, expanding progressively, which Adam identified as the "Roman climax in architecture", and which was to provide inspiration for his own mould-breaking designs.

At the time of his visit to Spalatro, the basement level of the palace was full of debris and it was not easy to explore the vast vaulted spaces on which the palace structure depended. The plan they produced was largely accurate, except that Adam thought the Emperor's Mausoleum to be the Temple of Jupiter, and the real Temple of Jupiter to be the Temple of Aesculapius. Considering Diocletian's earlier persecution of the Christians in Rome it seems fitting that his Mausoleum was later to form the medieval Cathedral of Spalatro.

The publication of Adam's study of the ruins of Spalatro, with drawings produced in Venice as well as in London, was intended as a self-advertisement, but by the time of its publication in 1764, the business of the Adam brothers had already taken off and the study was superfluous.

The Adam brothers' decision to set up in London was never going to be easy. They understood the need to have "a good address" to attract the clients who would be able to afford their services. Robert leased a house at 75 Lower Grosvenor Street and summoned two of his sisters, Jenny and Betty from Scotland, to manage his London establishment, which they seemed very happy to do. Luckily his consignment of Roman purchases had arrived at about the same time and he was therefore able to furnish his house and casino showroom with an impressive collection of Old Masters and antique fragments.

Mestrovic's Bishop of Nin sculpture (1930s) seems horrified by the advertising hoarding depicting the Golden gate of the Palace (2003)

The Peristyle before the Porticus, with the Mausoleum on the left (2003)

(both photos by Lester Borley)

In 1758 his first small commission was for an extension to General Bland's house in Isleworth, and he was beginning to be noticed and recommended. Lady Lindores introduced him to Edwin Lascelles, a member of the Society of Dilettanti, founded in London in 1732 for those who had been on the Grand Tour. Lascelles proposed to build a great house at Harewood in Yorkshire in which John Carr was already involved, but this became one of Robert Adam's influential commissions. He was then introduced to Sir Nathaniel Curzon of Kedleston which led to one of Adam's most significant projects, lasting several years.

The practice developed well and in the first ten years to 1768 had commissions stretching over several years from 42 clients, 20 of them in the London area. This was of course consistent with the prosperity which followed the Treaty of Paris in 1763 which ended the Seven Years War, and which brought not only political stability but also a crop of wealthy admirals and successful generals eager to spend their share of the spoils of war. At its peak the business of the Adam brothers employed 3000 workers

The project which caused the brothers the greatest financial loss was of course ironically the most advanced architecturally, the Adelphi Terrace on the banks of the River Thames. The Adam brothers had taken a 99-year lease in

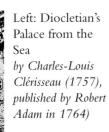

Left: Diocletian's Palace from the Sea
by Charles-Louis Clérisseau (1757), published by Robert Adam in 1764)

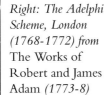

Right: The Adelphi Scheme, London (1768-1772) from The Works of Robert and James Adam *(1773-8)*

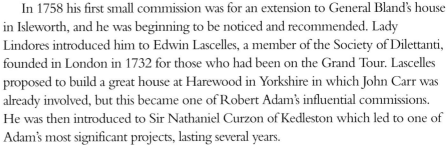

1768 from the Duke of St Albans on land which had belonged historically to the Bishops of Durham. The project was intended to transform a slum into a fashionable quarter and was the first attempt to construct houses in terraces, in two groups of eleven houses each back to back. Their friend, David Garrick, the actor, took one of the principal houses and the Adam family themselves lived in another. The best houses looked out onto an open terrace, clearly taking its inspiration from the cryptoporticus of Diocletian's Palace.

The land sloped steeply to the river, and to overcome the muddy foundations immense arched brick vaults were constructed, following the principles studied at Spalatro. It was hoped that the Government would take over the basement area as a store for the Ordnance Department, but this was not to be, and coupled with the collapse of a bank in 1772, the Adam brothers took a considerable loss, and they were forced to set up a Lottery for the unsold property with 108 prizes, which attracted 4370 investors at £50 apiece, which helped to salvage some of their outlay. (The Adam brothers themselves held a winning ticket).

The Adelphi Terrace was demolished in 1936, when there was an auction of ceilings painted by Angelika Kaufmann and Cipriani, and mantelshelves designed by Robert Adam. The drawing room of Garrick's house was reconstructed in the Victoria & Albert Museum. At 8 John Adam Street, the building designed for the Royal Society of Arts still stands as a fine example of their ambitious essay in urban planning.

In 1777 the 10th Earl of Cassilis commissioned Robert Adam to improve his property on the Ayrshire coast, a project which was to last until 1792. Culzean was a jumble of buildings set on a 300-foot sea cliff facing west towards the Isle of Arran. The commission for the new castle was also to include many other buildings in the designed landscape, including the home farm, the stables, the walled gardens, the viaduct and other smaller features.

There are two elements of Adam's design for Culzean Castle which are outstanding. The first is the bold drum tower built on the very edge of the sea cliff, which includes a spectacular round saloon with all its elements in harmony, including the specially woven carpet, the detail of the ceiling, the fireplaces and furniture. By chance, Adam's finished sketch for the ceiling design was acquired at an auction some fifty years ago, which enabled the

Culzean Castle, Ayrshire, constructed between 1777 and 1792 for the 10th Earl of Cassilis (All photos NTS)

Pompeo Batoni (1707-1787) Sir Thomas Kennedy, 9th Earl of Cassilis, whose two Grand Tours influenced the design

The three-storey staircase in which the Corinthian and Tuscan orders are reversed to achieve a greater sense of height

The garden front of Culzean Castle seen across the viaduct from the 'ruined' arch

National Trust for Scotland to restore the original colour scheme. The other outstanding element was the staircase placed between the new drum tower and the refurbished older building. In the narrow space available Adam conceived an oval staircase three storeys in height, top lit by a cupola. By reversing the order of the capitals used on the upper and lower floors, he achieved an illusion of greater height.

Although the commission came from David, the 10th Earl of Cassilis, who had never travelled far, it was undoubtedly influenced by his brother, Sir Thomas Kennedy, the 9th Earl, who had cut quite a dash on his two Grand Tours, and whose personal knowledge of the sources for Adam's neoclassical style was decisive.

The Adam brothers received 119 commissions between 1768 and 1792, and although they maintained their drawing office in London, they were involved in no fewer than 35 other major commissions in Scotland, many of which took several years to complete. At Mellerstain, where Robert Adam took on the house originally started by his father, work began in 1770 and continued until 1778. Its library and music room are probably two of the finest Adam interiors to be found anywhere.

There were other large-scale projects in Scotland during this period, including the Register House in Edinburgh for the Government (1774) and the Town College (1789), which is probably the largest of his public buildings with a dark, brooding entrance worthy of a capriccio by Piranesi. In 1791 he began the design for Charlotte Square, which is the outstanding European example of urban design in neoclassical form, rivalled only by Place Stanislas in Nancy, Lorraine.

Because of the overcrowding of the old town of Edinburgh, a competition was mounted to expand the city, and the winning plan was that created by the young architect James Craig, who is not known for much else. Craig's plan took many years to realise but was facilitated by the construction of the North Bridge which led to the completion of St Andrew's Square by 1781.

However the westward realisation towards what was St George's Square (later re-named Charlotte Square) took another ten years. Robert Adam was asked to produce a scheme for Charlotte Square, which was "not to be too extravagant" and for which he was paid £200. His concept was to group individual houses within a coherent external design on each of the four sides of the large square, focused on the domed structure of St George's Church which was to counter-balance St Andrew's Church in St Andrew's Square at the other end of George Street (which was never realised).

When Adam died at his London home in March 1792, he had eight public works and no less than 25 private buildings in hand, mainly in Scotland. Charlotte Square was one of these, and within days of his death the feus of the north side were offered for sale. Over the years the external appearance of individual houses was modified to suit the changing social needs of the occupants, and therefore the coherence of Adam's design was blurred. Between 1924 and 1927 the 4th Marquess of Bute undertook to restore the details of the north side of Charlotte Square to Adam's original elevations, by removing dormer windows and reverting all the windows to their original proportions.

Adam's concept of the palace front, embracing a group of individual houses, was to be used to great effect by later architects in Queen Street and Moray Place.

The publication between 1777 and 1778 of the fine series of folio engravings of the *Works in Architecture of Robert and James Adam* were of course intended to promote more work, and they remain an outstanding record of their *gesamtkunstwerk* approach to handling commissions for their clients. The Adam brothers' reputation went into decline in the early nineteenth century, when there was a taste for the emerging Greek Revival movement.

After the death of Robert Adam, the Board of Manufacturers in Edinburgh were offered but declined to purchase the office collection of 9,000 Adam drawings. They were snapped up in 1833 by Sir John Soane for £200 at auction. If one wishes to study the creative output of these most influential of architects, one must visit the Sir John Soane's house at 13 Lincoln's Inn Field in London, which is now a fascinating museum.

There was an Adam Revival in the late 19th century, and in 1879 the London-based interior decorators, Wright and Mansfield, used the style for the redecoration of Haddo House in Aberdeenshire.. When the 4th Marquess of Bute purchased No 5 Charlotte Square in at the beginning of the 20th century, Lady Bute had the ceiling of the drawing room recreated by the Scott Morton Company from an Adam design at Luton Hoo which she admired when they had lived there. Neoclassical design in the so-called "Adam style" continues to appeal.

Register House, Edinburgh (1774)
Engraving by Thomas Shepherd (1829)

The Town's College, Edinburgh (1789)
Engraving by Thomas Shepherd (1829)
(both engravings collection of Lester Borley)

The north side of Charlotte Square,
Edinburgh (1792) as restored 1924 - 1927
by the 4th Marquess of Bute
(National Trust for Scotland)

Dr Lester Borley CBE

Following a career developing British cultural tourism in the USA, Australia and Germany, he became successively Chief Executive of the statutory Scottish and English Tourist Boards. He then became Director of the National Trust for Scotland and subsequently Secretary General of Europa Nostra.

West side of Charlotte Square, Edinburgh, elevation by Robert Adam (1791), as part of the commision for the overall design for Charlotte Square

(National Trust for Scotland)

Perhaps the Encyclopaedia Britannica may have the last word on Robert Adam. "From façade to fire-irons, from chimneys to carpets, everything originated in the same order of ideas, and to this day an Adam drawing room is to English what a Louis Seize room is to French art".

List of sources

Robert Adam and his circle, John Fleming, John Murray 1962

The brothers Adam: the men and the style, Joseph and Anne Rykwert, Collins 1985 (which adopts the definitive list of Adam buildings compiled by Sir Howard Colvin)

Adam style, Steven Parissien, Phaidon 1992

Culzean and the Kennedy family, Michael Moss, Edinburgh University Press 2002

Bob the Roman (catalogue), Alistair Rowan, Sir John Soane's Museum 2003

Report of young heritage professionals' project in Split, Lester Borley, Europa Nostra 2003

Robert Adam, Richard Tames, Lifelines: Shire Books 2004

Monticello, in Charlottesville, Virginia, displays an innovative combination of Palladian, Neoclassical, and Thomas Jefferson's own designs.

Neoclassicism in the New World

The Influence of Thomas Jefferson and Benjamin Henry Latrobe

***John H. Stubbs, World Monuments Fund
and Columbia University, New York***

Introduction

*The influential Roman temple of
Maison Carrée in Nîmes published by
C.L. Clérisseau in 1778.*

The term 'tastemaker' has always had special meaning in the new world of the United States of America, a country that was completely developed in the modern sense in only a few hundred years. From colonial times through the 19th century in the United States individuals possessing rarified sensibilities in the arts, literature, history and philosophy often saw it as their duty to 'civilize' their surroundings. Among their many other accomplishments both Thomas Jefferson in his role of *amateur* architect, and professional architect and engineer Benjamin Henry Latrobe were tastemakers who introduced concepts and popularized highly influential new architecture in their time. After their long and illustrious careers both died in the 1820's having raised the stakes in architecture and its allied arts in ways that are evident today.

To appreciate their accomplishments one must imagine the physical and cultural contexts of Jefferson's and Latrobe's times. The so-called 'peopling' of America is not only the story of one of the greatest human migrations in history; it offers amazing stories about the transmission of ideas. Indeed the building of the nation's character is a story of the transplantation of life ways and the more useful of ideas from Old World to the New; their adaptation, and beyond that, invention.

The phenomenal growth of the United States from precarious early settlements along the Atlantic seaboard in the 16th century to the birth of the nation after independence in 1776, to a world power less than two centuries later is, it must be said, an astonishing thing. The reasons for this in large measure are due to the country's early settlers who were established and by the late 18th century. Most found themselves creators of a new nation, complete with its own representational government; one that fostered and claimed to guarantee economic, religious, and political freedom for all. The *tabula rasa* situation of a large land, rich in resources, which stood to be 'discovered' and exploited, instilled in many that arrived a sense of ambition, foresight, and a fervent belief in the future.

The period in America from the end of Revolution forward, when the new Republic was truly on its own, was all about consolidation and development. For those with skills and wit and who worked hard, the United States was a land of opportunity. Another late 18th century luminary, Benjamin Franklin, advised in his popular *Poor Richard's Almanac* "Chance favors the prepared mind". And, there is the contemporaneous epithet: "I will be a farmer, so my son can be a lawyer, so his son can be an artist." [1]

The population of the United States in 1800 was only 5.3 million people, and its key cities were Boston, New York, Newport, Philadelphia, Charleston and Savannah. Other cities along North America's south coast such as Mobile and New Orleans were still in the hands of the Spanish or French. Everything west of the Mississippi River, save for the Spanish missions in the southwest and west coast north to San Francisco, California, was terra incognita; something that Jefferson capitalized upon on behalf of the United States in 1803 while serving as country's third President in 1803, when he purchased the vast Louisiana territory from France.

Such were some of the conditions and possibilities that Thomas Jefferson and Benjamin Henry Latrobe faced at the prime of their lives in the newly established United States of America. Granted Jefferson and Latrobe were no ordinary men. Each had such widely ranging interests and experiences that it is

Benjamin Henry Latrobe (1803) at the height of his career as America's first formally trained resident architect and enginee..

hard to limit discussion of their achievements in architecture. Adding to the challenge of distinguishing their specific achievements is the fact Jefferson's and Latrobe's lives intersected repeatedly from 1798 until the end of their lives through their interests in architecture and urban improvement schemes, and due to the rise in Jefferson's political fortunes.

In observing the careers of each man it is evident how their respective tenures in Europe greatly affected their world views, interests and talents as architects. Latrobe was sent to learn and support himself while doing so. Jefferson was sent to Paris as an emissary of the United States with official duties. It is the travelling that both did while on the Continent that we refer to here as their 'Grand Tours' for the purposes of this paper.[2]

Benjamin Henry Latrobe

Benjamin Henry Latrobe was born in Leeds, England in 1764. From his youth he showed an interest in architecture and drawing and at the age of 12 he was sent to the Continent to study at the Moravian Pedagogium at Niesky in German Silesia. His education appears to have been directed at the ministry but while still in Germany Latrobe showed an interest in engineering, observing the levee systems and flood control works along the Elbe and other rivers. Much of his final year abroad was spent traveling in Germany, France, and Italy on a trip that strengthened his idea of becoming an architect and that also influenced his later works. Latrobe returned to England in 1784 an accomplished mathematician, linguist, musician, watercolorist, writer, and advocate of political and social reform. After a brief stay as a clerk in the Stamp Office in London, Latrobe worked in the offices of John Smeaton and Samuel Pepys Cockerell, designer of the Admiralty Building at Whitehall, a project that Latrobe worked on.[3]

During the years of his European education and travel, Latrobe was undoubtedly impressed with the new classicism of the time as exemplified in the works of Claude Nicholas Ledoux, Etienne Louis Boullée and a host of others in France, and Karl Gottfried Langhans in Silesia. According the American restoration architect and architectural historian Samuel Wilson Jr., nothing in European architecture probably influenced Latrobe more than the Francophile style of John Soane.[4] Soane's special treatment of solid geometrical forms in architecture and masterful designs for light and shadow characterized the new architecture of the end of the eighteenth century and were to become elements in Latrobe's own design concepts.

Conditions in Labtrobe's life after the loss of his wife in 1793, coupled with political unrest and a slowing of the economy associated with French Revolution, were such that he decided to seek a new life and career in the United States arriving in Virginia in 1796. Against the advice of many of his friends Latrobe chose the New World.

He arrived in Norfolk, Virginia at the mouth of the James River where his charming personality, knowledge, and enthusiasm won him friends from the start. His keen observations and sketches of the people and places in his adopted new home serve to this day as prime historical sources.[5] Latrobe later moved to Richmond, Virginia, where he lived for seven years and designed several houses with his most famous building being the Richmond Penitentiary (1797) which included some of the most advanced ideas of Thomas Jefferson's concept of humane penology.[6]

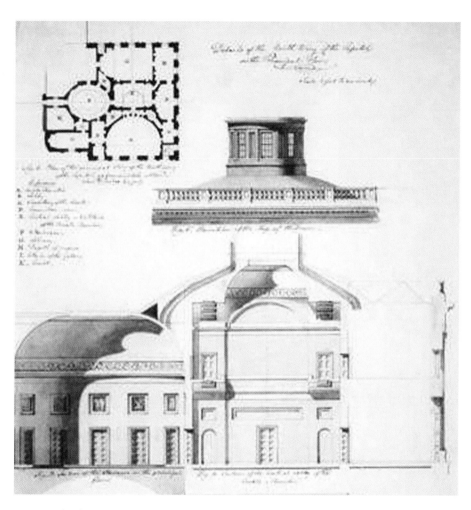

Latrobe's drawings for the Bank of Pennsylvania (1799), a design which heralded the Greek Revival style for institutional buildings thereafter.

Latrobe later moved to Philadelphia with his appointment as architect for the newly established Bank of Pennsylvania (1799). The bank project stood as a uniquely grand conception for a building of this type at the time in America. The circular banking room was contained within a central cubical mass, surrounded by a low dome and lighted from above by a handsome cupola. Six-columned Ionic porticos extended from the front and rear, setting a precedent for countless Greek Revival porticoes that followed.[7]   The bank also

107

The pumping facilities of Latrobe's Philadelphia Water Works (foreground).

contained the first masonry vaulted monumental interior in the United States. Latrobe's design for this impressive and sizable building established him as the most competent architect in the United States.

Latrobe's other major Philadelphia work was as engineer and architect for the Philadelphia Water Works (1799). He proposed the use of steam engines to raise the water from the Schuylkill River to a high point in the city, distributing it from a reservoir by an elaborate piping system. Much of the Waterworks complex survives today with its handsome and highly literate

Opposite: Latrobe's Roman Catholic Cathedral (1804 1818), Baltimore, Maryland.

classical revival detailing.

Latrobe's Philadelphia Water Works project, eventually led him to his last architectural commission some nearly 20 years later in New Orleans where with Thomas Jefferson's strong encouragement he again designed water pumping and distribution system for an entire city. In between these ambitious engineering works, Latrobe designed a number of other structures. One was in the role as Surveyor of the Public Buildings of the United States, as appointed by President Thomas Jefferson, where he was charged with the completion of the construction of the new nation's Capitol building. In this project he had the difficult task of revising designs for the building by William Thornton which were in the process of being built, an interruption of affairs which led to bitter feelings between the two. Latrobe persevered and his attention to the project over a fourteen year period (1803-1817) led to the great architect's chief 'claim to fame'. During the long Capitol construction project he advised and worked with Thomas Jefferson on a variety of other projects, most notably Jefferson's own proudest architectural achievement, the University of Virginia.

Latrobe had his frustrations with the Capitol project. He was criticized all along by William Thornton, who also sued him, and was hurt by Washington politicians undervalued his efforts. A letter from Latrobe to Jefferson reveals this sensitivity. In it Latrobe comments on the popularity of one of his designs, the 'Americanization' of the corinthinan column capitals in the Senate Chamber stair vestibule (now Statuary Hall), where he replaced acanthus leaves with a native corn motif. He wrote: "this capital….obtained me more applause from the members of Congress than all the works of magnitude…They call it the Corn Cob Capital." [8]

Through the admiration of Thomas Jefferson and others Latrobe worked on other projects in Washington D.C. including improvements to the White House, and the construction of buildings on nearby Lafayette Square.

Another of Latrobe's greatest architectural achievements was his design for the first Roman Catholic Cathedral in the United States (1804-1818). Its glory is its low domed sixty-foot wide rotunda opening

designed to illuminate the interior with indirect light, an idea borrowed from both French and Soanian examples. What was distinctive however was Latrobe's design of the structure of the dome; an ingenious double dome having an inner construction of brick and stone that was covered by an outer wooden shell with a ten foot gap in between. The structure of the cathedral structure in general also cleverly engineered using a series of radial vaults to transfer the dome's tensile stress to an abutment below which was set into walls that were supported by inverted arches at the foundation level.[9] Without a doubt it represents the thinking of a seriously capable engineer and architect.[10]

Benjamin Henry Latrobe is a good example of an architect who was influential in his own time; in this instance almost to an extreme. He wearied at the extent to which his work was being copied. He wrote in 1812, in reference to other builders in Philadelphia copying his Greek revival designs, "I have changed the taste of whole city. My very follies and faults and whims have been mimicked." [11]

It's worth recalling here that a good client can be as, or even more, influential than their architect. For instance, it was the influential Pennsylvania banker Nicholas Biddle who more than any other who made Greek Revival popular throughout the country.[12] Biddle's own Grand Tour, that included Rome and Greece, left him with the belief that Classical Revival, especially the Greek Revival, was the only proper style for America's institutional buildings.

Latrobe produced designs for numerous other American buildings, most of which were never realized, and, unfortunately, the majority of his built works were demolished. Nonetheless, through his associations with others who built and through the impressions his architecture made, he had a lasting influence. He is credited above all else for creating public architecture which was entirely different from domestic architecture. The building types with which he was associated were as varied as their locations–libraries, banks, offices, exchanges, capitol buildings, churches, residences–in Virginia, Maryland, Washington, DC, Pennsylvania, Kentucky, Tennessee, and New Orleans.

In November 1817 after one last battle in Washington over his U.S. Capitol building project, Latrobe moved to Baltimore and later relocated to New Orleans to oversee one of his several projects there, the first being a new

Thomas Jefferson while Secretary of State, December 1791.
Portrait by Charles Willson Peale.

(Courtesy of Independence National Park).

Custom House.[13] The physical challenges associated with his last project-plans to design, finance, build, and operate the waterworks for New Orleans, led to his end. In early September 1820 while overseeing construction of the waterworks he contracted yellow fever and died.

Despite his disappointments, through his enthusiasm for building and diligence Benjamin Henry Latrobe did succeed in the greatest of his aspirations: laying the foundations of professional architecture in America. This is evidenced by one of his pupils and assistants, Robert Mills, who himself later claimed to be the first professionally trained architect in America.[14]

The American architectural historian Roger Kennedy probably describes Latrobe's achievements best he when he calls Latrobe "the greatest figure in the first three generations of American architecture." [15]

Thomas Jefferson

Thomas Jefferson was born in 1743 at the edge of western settlement in America in what is now Albemarle County, Virginia. His father was a 'gentleman justice' and surveyor who married well leaving Thomas Jefferson, his eldest son, about five thousand acres and an established position. With an interest during this youth in mathematics and exploration and an exposure to Latin and Greek languages he entered the College of William and Mary in Williamsburg, Virginia in March 1760 where he keenly pursued the classics, philosophy, the natural sciences and law. As a student in Williamsburg, the then-capital of the English colonies, on the eve of the American Revolution Jefferson was well placed as a witness to history in the making.

He married in 1772 and had six children with only two surviving to maturity. The family home that he called Monticello was located some 120 miles west of Williamsburg. He designed it himself, primarily using Palladio's *Four Books* as a source for a number of its details, especially its primary and garden facades. Monticello was built on a small mountaintop that overlooked the town of Charlottesville. It was a working plantation, that was largely self-sustaining, that was carefully operated by a young Jefferson who from 1760 progressed from being appointed county lieutenant of Albemarle to a member of the House of Burgesses in Williamsburg.

From his well-placed social and political position, Thomas Jefferson diligently participated in the legal machinations of his time. In 1774 he published paper entitled A Summary View of the Rights of British America and his drafting of the Declaration of Independence are his greatest contributions to the American Revolution.

Jefferson's third notable literary achievement was his *Notes on the State of Virginia* that described everything about the land, its economy, its people, and even the life ways and monumental remains of Native Americans in the region. His *Notes* were eventually published Paris in 1785 partly to combat the theories of Buffon and Raynal who had concluded that both animal and intellectual life in America was inferior.[16] Jefferson's work on this publication over a period of several years did much to establish his contemporary reputation as a universal scholar and a pioneer American scientist.

The tumultuous Revolutionary War years that lasted for nearly five years finally ended with independence for the thirteen colonies and the start of a new period; the building of the nation. The diplomatic needs of the young country were pressing in the years that followed and in May 1784 Jefferson was

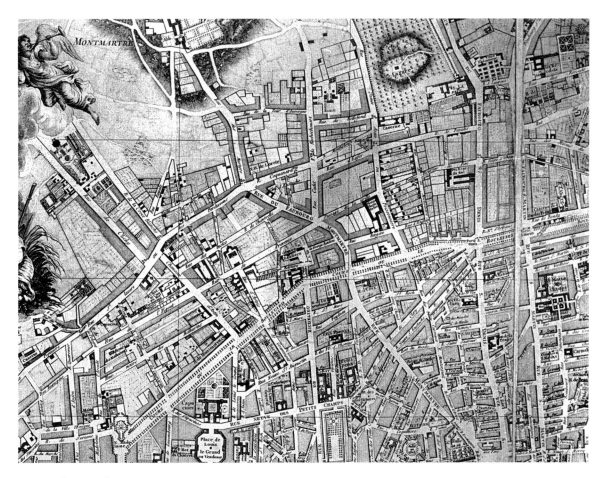

Paris at the time of Thomas Jefferson's stay, 1784-1789.

sent to Paris to join Benjamin Franklin and John Adams negotiating commerce treaties and similar matters from the position of France, the most supportive of America's allies in its struggles against the British. He was said to have fit in well as an American *savant* in Paris under the towering figures of his predecessor Benjamin Franklin, and the Compte de Lafayette, who were seen as heroes of the American Revolution.

As for the term Grand Tour and how it applied to Thomas Jefferson, in a sense, his whole tenure in Europe from 1784 to 1789 was one long Grand

Tour. From the start he was enamored by Paris, and intensely pursued its intellectual offerings. Fluent in French, and three other languages, he enthusiastically participated in a wide range of social and intellectual worlds, including the art world, at the height of the Ancien Régime absorbing all that he could.

Jefferson took advantage of a diplomatic mission to England in 1786 to see its great gardens and planned landscapes. He and John Adams visited numerous notable eighteenth century sites, including at Windsor Castle and Blenheim Palace, and the great houses and pleasure gardens at Chiswick and Stowe.

The following year on his doctor's recommendation in order to cure a broken wrist, he took an extended tour to the south of France and northern Italy. He spent nearly fifteen weeks tirelessly visiting dozens of towns and cities and sites. He rarely stopped at a place for more than one night, and saw Nice, Lyons, Aix-en-Provence, before crossing the Alps to visit Turin, Milan and Genoa. Duties called back at his post so after viewing agricultural production in the Genoa region he returned to Paris, promising himself he would return some day and continue on.

What he did see on this mission proved to be enough…. In Provence he visited the Pont du Gard and the arch and arena of Orange, calling them "superb". In 1788, a third European mission from Paris took him to Amsterdam to complete a large loan to the United States, and he traveled through parts of Germany and the Netherlands.

Of the various places Jefferson's saw as American plenipotentiary to Europe, Paris left the deepest impression. He found the place congenial; its people, salons, galleries, book shops and gardens sophisticated and stimulating. Jefferson immediately found old buildings to admire. The city itself was a virtual construction site with the visionary architects Ledoux and Boulle bringing a fresh slant to classical antiquity. The Rotonde de Monceau, one of Ledoux's *barrieres* of Paris particularly inspired Jefferson, the amateur architect. In France he saw Roman architecture filtered through neoclassical ideals and how it could serve its modern users. He was fascinated by the aims of rational purity that Neoclassicism offered.

Other buildings found themselves in his architectural imagination, including the Halle aux Bleds with its dome construction and skylights by Phillibert Delorme, and

The Rotonde de Monceau, one of several of Claude Nicholas Ledoux's designs which inspired the architectural ideals of Thomas Jefferson.

especially a house under construction at the time, the Hôtel de Salm by Pierre Rousseau, with which Jefferson found himself, he said: "violently smitten." [17] A grand private home with a central dome, the Hôtel de Salm proved to be the single most important inspiration for his reinvention of Monticello on his return to America, just as a plate in Palladio's *Four Books* has been for the earlier Monticello.

Jefferson was amazed by Le Desert de Retz, Racine de Monville's fantastic house outside Paris which had been built to look like an enormous broken four-story fluted column in ruins. He was especially taken by the ingenious way its elliptical rooms had been fitted into its circular plan.

He eagerly pursued the art world when time making sure to attend the fall exhibitions at the salons of the Louvre. Of the exposition of 1787, he wrote to his friend John Trumball, then in London:

"The salon has been open four or five days. I inclose you list of it's treasures. [seen here] The best thing is the Death of Socrates by David, and a superb one it is. A crucifixion by Roland in imitation of Relief is as perfect as it can be. Five pieces of antiquities by Robert are among the foremost. Many portraits of Madme. Lebrun are exhibited and much approved. There are (an) abundance of things in the stile of mediocrity. Upon the whole it is well worth your coming to see. You have only to get into the Diligence and in 4 days you are here." [18]

He goes on to describe a very different Louvre that we the one we know today. The Royal Academy of Painting and Sculpture and the Royal Academy of Architecture had its headquarters there. Artists' studios and lodgings were found in the various odd corners of the building, especially in it upper reaches, and even in attics. It was considered great good fortune for an artist to obtain an apartment in the Louvre. Several of the painters with whose work Jefferson became acquainted lived in the Cour du Louvre including Hubert Robert, and Clérisseau.[19]

He pursued the arts to the extent that he bought at auction, and acquired books on the average of one per day. His extensive diaries and some of his later writings tell of his observations and purchases. After returning to America he described his method of purchasing books to a friend:

"While residing in Paris, I devoted every afternoon I was disengaged, for a summer or two, in examining all the principal bookstores, turning over every book with my own hand, and putting by everything which related to America, and indeed whatever was rare and valuable in every science. Besides this, I had standing orders during the whole time I was in Europe, on its principal book-marts, particularly in Amsterdam, Frankfort, Madrid and London, for such work relating to America as could not be found in Paris." [20]

Inspired by French and Italian architecture Thomas Jefferson constantly considered its possible applications in America. While in Paris he produced a design for the President's House in Washington (never built) that appears to have been primarily inspired by the illustration of the Villa Rotunda in the Leoni edition of Palladio's *The Four Books*.

Jefferson was also deeply interested all aspects of the *jardin anglais* that he had seen in Paris and its environs, and the park designs he noticed on his tours. The French formal parks intrigued him also, which may well have been an inspiration for the layout of one of two of his most famous architectural works, the Academical Village of the University of Virginia. He certainly found his knowledge of French formal gardens and grand planning useful later during his presidency while working with Pierre L'Enfant on a new plan for Washington, D.C.

Jefferson's five years in France were the happiest period of his life. His eclectic and imaginative mind was open to new ideas that he encountered in Paris on the eve of great change that was soon to occur there. On his departure from Paris on 26 September 1789 he had planned to return to Europe to see more, especially Italy and beyond, but demands on his abilities at home and conditions in Europe were to provide a new phase of his life. As for the artistic side of Thomas Jefferson, one can only imagine how his seeing Rome and Greece first hand would have further shaped his architectural abilities and ambitions.

Jefferson's Architecture

The Capitol of Virginia in Richmond

In 1785 while in France Jefferson received a letter from the Directors of public buildings in Virginia asking him to procure a plan for a new Capitol planned for Richmond.[21] Jefferson's response is best summarized in a letter he wrote to James Madison referring to the matter where he said: "I shall send the one (a design) taken from the best morsel of 'antient' architecture now

The new Capitol in Richmond, Virginia, based on the Maison Carré, Nîmes (engraving, c.1820).

remaining." He was referring to the Maison Carrée in Nîmes which the celebrated teacher and architectural renderer Charles-Louis Clérisseau had recently published in several plates within his *Antiquités de la France* (1778).

Jefferson befriended Clérisseau and together they worked out a plan for the capitol that took into account the functions that had to be accommodated. In negotiating the design it was probably Jefferson who changed the Orders from Corinthian as found on Maison Carrée to Ionic, on account of the difficulty of the Corinthian capitals. Except for the change to the Ionic Order, the insertion of windows, chimneys, and its floor plans within, the completed Virginia Capitol building bore a remarkable resemblance to its ancient prototype although it was twice as large. (Out of necessity for additional space the Capitol was enlarged with recessed wings set behind smaller Ionic porticos in 1904, and again enlarged in an extensive restoration-expansion completed in 2007 that entailed new meeting halls, circulation and reception facilities in excavated areas underground in front of the Capitol building.)

In his own Account of the Capitol of Virginia Thomas Jefferson cites: "the Capitol in the city of Richmond . . . is (based) on the model of the temples of Erectheus at Athens, and of Balbec, and of the Maison quarree at Nismes, all of which are nearly of the same form & proportion and are considered as the most perfect examples of Cubic architecture, as the Pantheon of Rome is of the Spherical." [23]

Due largely to the time it took to correspond in the late eighteenth century and probably due to political machinations associated with the project at the time, work on a different design for the Capitol building began any way, which so disturbed Jefferson that he managed to have the work stopped. Among the letters Jefferson wrote, urging delay until the plans should arrive from abroad were a variety of justifications for the new design. In one he wrote to James Madison on 1 September 1785 encouraging the Directors of Public Buildings to wait he writes: "It will be superior in beauty to anything in America, and not inferior to anything in the world." [24]   He mentions in passing in another letter to Madison on 20 September when explaining how he (and Clérisseau) took for their model "the most beautiful and precious morsel of architecture left to us by antiquity-the Maison Carré-built by Caius and Lucius Caesar and repaired by Louis XIV." He further describes how "It is very simple, but it is noble beyond expression and would have done honour to our country as presenting to travelers a morsel of taste in our infancy promising much for our maturer age." [25]

As for the specific design of the building, Jefferson took a leading role in the process, negotiating certain details with Clérisseau who produced several of the drawings and who arranged for a scale model of the building to be fabricated by one of the best modelures of the time (Jean-Pierre Fouquet). The details of Jefferson's procurement of Clérriseau's help and those of the model makers are well documented in Jefferson's correspondence. ….From their correspondence it is clear how the model forced many design decisions, how long it took to make, its cost (15 guineas or 1 louie), and even how it was packed for shipping to Richmond from Paris for eventual display in a glass case.[26] This is the earliest-known and probably the first architectural model for an American building.

Continuing on the question of authorship, Clérisseau was certainly responsible for the official set of drawings sent to Richmond and various refinements to the design, though the choice of Maison Carrée as the principal design source, the concept of fitting the Capitol functions in to a prismatic temple form, the layout of interior spaces, and the insistence on using this design for the new Richmond statehouse were Jefferson's.[27]

Design sources for the Capitol in Richmond in the form pattern books certainly include: Clérisseau's *Antiquities of France; Monuments of Nîmes* and Palladio's *Architecture of A. Palladio; in Four Books*, in particular, its *Book IV*. Other works probably consulted include both Julien-David Le Roy's and James Stuart and Nicholas Revett's competing works on the buildings of Athens, Claude Perrault's edition of Vitruvius, and Robert Wood's books on Baalbek and Palmyra.[28]

The entrance elevation of Monticello which is harmonious with the villa's garden elevation.

In all this mention of sources and influences, it is important to understand that Jefferson's intention at the Capitol in Richmond was not just about styling for the sake of appearances. It was about symbolism and inspiration. At the centre of its 36-foot square double-height central hall which is topped by a cylindrical dome was placed Jean-Antoine Houdon's likeness of George Washington, who even during the general's lifetime, was seen without a doubt as *the* hero of the country since he gave its citizens liberty. The temple-like Capitol building was the only solution for such a shrine of honor.

Monticello

In 1793, at the end of his service as Secretary of State, Jefferson was fifty-one years old. Though his wife and four of his six children had died, Jefferson decided to enlarge Monticello. He had returned from Europe a confirmed Francophile, loaded with furniture and accessories, a French cook, French wine, and the latest books on European architecture.

At Monticello Jefferson decided to imitate, at least in part, the relatively small and *chic* Hôtel de Salm with its central dome and projecting salon. This design for a residential building resulted in an image without parallel for its period in the United States. The image in fact endures; practically every American carries with them daily an image of Monticello's garden elevation on the nickel coin, with Jefferson's portrait on the verso.

The U-shaped plan of Monticello is very Palladian as one readily sees on viewing plans of the house and on visiting it his original drawings for the house, though Jefferson cleverly built the cellar levels of enveloping wings on the building's garden elevation into the brow of the hill on which the house is situated. As with Palladio's villas, everything necessary for operating such an estate had its place.

Monticello's rooms at the ground level are mostly irregular in shape and are handsomely detailed. Circulation at this *piano nobile* level is both axial and by means of a secondary circuit of openings in rooms forming the perimeter of the house. Jefferson's famous bedroom-study incorporates two rooms with differing functions; his library and writing areas. Two of

The south section of the eastern colonnade forming the Lawn of the University of Virginia.

Monticello's most elegant rooms are the dining room and its adjacent projecting salon, or drawing room. The salon projects under the garden front portico and is topped by the dome. The accommodation of specialized designs of rooms all having a harmonious décor of spare classical detailing well reveal the abilities of its famous builder and owner as a competent and imaginative architectural designer. The fact that both principal facades have impressive porticoed entrances of differing designs, each accessible by driveways (now pathways), also reveals Jefferson's interest in maximizing space efficiency and his fascination with the symbolic and exemplary roles of classical architecture.

Thomas Jefferson's enthusiasm for architecture was well known among his peers and he found himself frequently consulted by others. He is the sole designer of several other houses in Virginia, including his second home Poplar Forest (1806) near Lynchburg, and there are attributions of his input at many more.[29]

The University of Virginia

Jefferson had been contemplating ideas for creating a university since at least January 1800. From 1817 to 1826 his plan was realized. He is attributed as the architect of its complete design from its grand concept as an arrangement of ten pavilions, of differing neoclassical designs that line both sides of the university's great Lawn, to the plans and specific details of each, to the lower garden areas to the rear of each pavilion.[30]

The Rotunda at the head of the ensemble originally held the university's library and, as at Monticello, is raised above a service level and is double-facing. Its shape and size derive from the ideal example of 'spherical architecture' as Jefferson called it, Hadrian's Pantheon in Rome.[31] The main floor of the Rotunda originally consisted of an arrangement of three great oval rooms that were joined by an hour-glass shaped hall which was lost in a disastrous fire in 1895 and not properly restored to their original design until 1976.[32]

As amazing is the arrangement of the ten elegant neoclassical pavilions and their adjacent spaces that originally served as teaching facilities and living quarters for students and their instructors of philosophy, the sciences, the arts. No two pavilions are alike and each serves as an exemplar for teaching the Orders.

The most advanced design was inspired not by an ancient form but likely by the Hôtel Guimard in Paris that Jefferson found to be especially appealing. (Interestingly on Jefferson's drawing of Pavilion IX is written in Jefferson's hand is written "Latrobe", suggesting that Latrobe supplied the design.) Other designs for the pavilion facades were based on architectural pattern books including details from the Baths of Diocletian, the temple of Fortuna Virilis (Portunus), and the Theater of Marcellus.

For this last and greatest of all of his architectural accomplishments Jefferson sought the advice of William Thornton and Latrobe each of whom were helpful. It

Thomas Jefferson designed the Rotunda as the library and central feature of his "academical village" concept.

was Thornton, for instance, who suggested that the distances between the pavilions along both sides of the Lawn be increased in their relation to one another in the southerly direction.

Thomas Jefferson's believe that properly designed and built classical architecture was critical to the higher education of young Americans was also exemplified in his retaining two Italian sculptors to carve the Corinthian capitals at the University.[33] The commitment to quality, the originality of the designs of both Monticello and the Academical Village of University of Virginia, and their influence, merited the listing of both on UNESCO's World Heritage list in 1987.

Conclusion

It is remarkable that both Jefferson's and Latrobe's enormous contributions to American architecture were based on the architecture of ancient Greece and Rome located half way around the world. Their motives and means were not dissimilar to those responsible for the "Athens of the North" – Edinburgh, or its counterpart Neoclassical architectural marvels in Germany, Sweden and Russia.

Both Thomas Jefferson and Benjamin Henry Latrobe saw it as their task to help civilize a then rough, newly-established United States of America. Both were well positioned to do so, and both well understood the power of example. Through their passion, hard work, and considerable achievements in introducing literate and imaginative Neoclassical architecture to the New World – that would later be called by some America's "national architecture" – they stand among the most important of all Americans.

Acknowledgements

The author wishes to thank the State Archives Department of the Library of Virginia for its generous assistance for receiving me at the Capitol at Richmond on 24 August 2007, when a wealth of information and illustrations relative to the architectural history of the Capitol building was made available. This meeting was organized by Dr. George Skarmeas of RMJM Hillier Planners of Philadelphia, restoration architects for the Capitol, in cooperation with Calder Loth, architectural historian for the Virginia Department of Historic Resources, who generously

The Tuscan, Ionic and Corinthian orders on three (of ten) pavilions facing the Lawn served as exemplars for education in the 'classics'.

organized this introduction and the availability of illustrative material. Gratitude is also extended to Michael Schuller of Atkinson-Noland & Associates, Engineers of Boulder, Colorado and Jack Waite Associates Architects, Albany, New York, for technical diagrams and information on the structural designs of Latrobe's Roman Catholic Basilica in Baltimore, Maryland. Images on pages 51, 54 and 65 were sourced on the World Wide Web. Images on pages 53 and 55 courtesy: Library of Congress. The contemporary images here were provided by the author, and the portrait of Thomas Jefferson provided courtesy of National Park Service, Museum Management Program and Independence National Historical Park, Philadelphia. www.cr.nps.gov/museum

Bibliography

Adams, William Howard (ed.). *The Eye of Jefferson*. Thomas Jefferson Memorial Foundation, Inc. Charlottesville, Va. 1976.

Bergh, Albert Ellery (ed.). *The Writings of Thomas Jefferson* Washington, D.C.: Issued under the Auspices of the Thomas Jefferson Memorial Association of the United States, 1903, letter from Thomas Jefferson to James Madison, 20 Sept. 1785, 8:534-535.

Hafertepe, Kenneth and James F O'Gorman, (eds.). *American Architects and Their Books to 1848*. University of Massachusetts Press, Amherst, MA. 2001. (especially the articles by Richard Guy Wilson entitled "Thomas Jefferson's 'bibliomanie' and Architecture" and Jeffrey Cohen's "The Architectural Libraries of Benjamin Henry Latrobe.")

Kennedy, Roger. *Architecture, Men, Women and Money 1600-1860*. Random House, NY, 1985.

Kimball, Sydney Fiske. *American Architecture*. Bobbs-Merrill Company, NY, 1928.

Kulka, Jon et al. (eds.) The Capitol of Virginia, *A Landmark of American Architecture by Fiske Kimball*. Library of Virginia, Richmond, 2002.

Lane, Mills. *Architecture of the Old South*. Beehive Press, Savannah, Georgia 1992.

Lehman, Karl. *Thomas Jefferson, American Humanist*. The Macmillan Company, NY. 1947.

Placzek, Adolf (ed.) *The MacMillan Encyclopedia of Architects*. New York, 1982. (Essays within by Samuel Wilson, Jr. on Benjamin Henry Latrobe and by Frederick Doveton Nichols on Thomas Jefferson.)

Malone, Dumas. *Thomas Jefferson; A Brief Biography*. Thomas Jefferson Memorial Foundation, University of North Carolina, reprint, 1986.

Nichols, Frederick Doveton. *Thomas Jefferson's Architectural Drawings.* 4th ed. Massachusetts Historical Society, Boston, 1978.

Nichols, Frederick Doveton and Ralph E. Griswold. *Thomas Jefferson, Landscape Architect.* University of Virginia Press, Charlottesville, 1978.

Rice, Howard C. *Thomas Jefferson's Paris.* Princeton University Press, Princeton, New Jersey, 1976.

Scully, Vincent. *American Architecture: Innovation and Tradition*, Rizzoli, New York, 1983.

Wilson, Richard Guy (ed.) *Thomas Jefferson's Academical Village, the Creation of an Architectural Masterpiece,* Barly Art Museum of the University of Virginia, Charlottesville 1994.

Notes and Sources

1 Benjamin Franklin, *The Writings of Benjamin Franklin; Poor Richard's Almanac,* Philadelphia, 1936.

2 Benjamin Henry Latrobe left the Old World for the New at age of 31 while Thomas Jefferson was a third-generation native-born American.

3 Samuel Wilson, Jr. "William Henry Latrobe" in *The Macmillan Encyclopedia of Architects.* The Free Press., New York, 1982, 611-12.

4 Ibid. 612.

5 Latrobe's sketches of the remains of Williamsburg, Virginia were of great assistance in the restoration of the colonial capital. Through his friendship with George Washington's nephew, he visited Mount Vernon, where there too, his sketches of the place proved invaluable in its famous restoration by public subscription in the 1850's.

6 Individual cells for prisoners, a novel concept at the time, were arranged around a large semicircular court. The last vestige of the Richmond Penitentiary was demolished in 1927.

7 The appeal of the temple front and the 'noble simplicity' (as Wincklemann termed it) of Greek architecture, often along with its idealized political associations had resonance in forward-looking democratic America. English architects including Stuart and Revett, Wilkins, Dance, Soane, and C. R. Cockerel authored the Greek Revival in architecture in England which with the help of

pattern books was expanded upon even further in examples of monumental classicism in Russia and in the American South.

8 Ibid. 613.

9 A version of this kind of foundation that post-dates this example is on display in the basement of St. George's Hall in Liverpool.

10 The full extent of Latrobe's ingenious engineering design to achieve span and special lighting effects at the Catholic Cathedral in Baltimore was fully realized only a few years ago in a restoration of the building.

11 Ibid. 613. Like the better architects of his period Latrobe was just as comfortable designing in the Roman and Gothic styles, as his favorite-the Greek Revival.

12 Roger Kennedy. *Architecture, Men, Women and Money 1600-1860.* Random House, New York, 1985.

13 In New Orleans Latrobe also built a church, several residences, and made major improvements to the *Place d' Arms* (Jackson Square).

14 Ibid. *Kennedy,* 320.

15 Ibid.

16 Howard C. Rice. *Thomas Jefferson's Paris.* Princeton University Press, 1976, 85.

17 Ibid. 10

18 Ibid, 33. Thomas Jefferson to John Trumball, 30 August 1787, Julian P. Boyd et al. (eds.) *The Papers of Thomas Jefferson* 12: 69, Princeton University Press.

19 Ibid., 32-33.

20 Jefferson to Samuel H. Smith, 21 September 1814 in Jefferson, *Writings,* 14:191. The surviving shipping lists for Jefferson's trip home revealed his love for acquiring things. Some 80 crates of French furniture were sent back.

21 The accounts of this correspondence are many and have drawn renewed scholarly interest in recent years.

22 Thomas Jefferson to James Madison, 1 September, 1785, in Boyd, *Jefferson Papers,* 8:462.

23 Fisk Kimball, *American Architecture*, Bobbs-Merrill Company, NY, 1928, xv.

24 Thomas Jefferson to James Madison, 1 September, 1785, in Boyd, *Jefferson Papers*, 8:462

25 Thomas Jefferson to James Madison, 20 September 1785, ibid. 8:462. (This reference to repairs to Maison Carrée during the Sun King's era helps place it as one of the first 'restorations for the sake of restoration' in Europe.)

26 The original Fouquet model was restored a few years ago by conservators at Colonial Williamsburg where depictions of early finishes, etc. were revealed in an exciting conservation project that merited a special conference of Jefferson scholars and technicians.

27 The Clérisseau drawings do not survive. The best summary of scholarly research on the Richmond Capitol building over the years, and a brilliant correction and synthesis of it, is found in a salutary re-appraisal entitled: *The Capitol of Virginia, A Landmark of American Architecture* by Fiske Kimball. Jon Kulka et al. (eds.) Library of Virginia, Richmond, 2002.

28 Thomas Jefferson's reference books played a key role in the design of the Richmond Capitol and all of his other architectural projects. The prominent architectural historian and University of Virginia professor Richard Guy Wilson figured that Jefferson amassed six libraries in his life, and always cherished his source book on architecture. In Wilson's "Thomas Jefferson's 'bibliomanie' and Architecture" within *American Architects and Their Books to 1848* (Kenneth M. Hafertepe and James F. O'Gorman, eds.), 2001 are found the sources and context of two of Jefferson's more notable quotes on the role of books; he referred to his various editions of Palladio as "the architectural Bible", and once wrote to John Adams saying "I cannot live without books."

29 Jefferson had an equal appreciation of the landscape; "Nature's work", as he called it. He was an accomplished horticulturalist and gardener, and frequently corresponded on botanical matters in assistance to others.

30 Though in his usual open-minded and inquiring fashion, Jefferson consulted others including Latrobe.

31 Jefferson had a deep interest in the symbolic value of round architecture, and its associations with Vitruvian proportion.

32 The prominent architect Stanford White renovated the Rotunda in 1895 fitting in an arrangement of rectilinear rooms. Jefferson's original design source of this suite of oval rooms was

Professor John H Stubbs

Vice President for Field Projects for the World Monuments Fund in New York, supervising conservation programmes at 250 sites in 86 countries, and also teaches Historic Preservation in the graduate programme of Columbia University, New York, as well as being Chairman of the James Marston Fitch Charitable Foundation.

likely based on Racine de Monville's eccentric Column House at Le Désert de Retz outside Paris that he is known to have visited.

33 Due to the quality of the local stone, this idea was soon abandoned; the sculptors were sent home, and the Corinthian and Ionic capitals of the Rotunda were imported from Carrara, Italy.

Syon House, details of the ante-room from
The Works of Robert and James Adam *(1773-8)*
Engraving by Giovanni Battista Piranesi

Karl Friedrich Schinkel, Cathedral on the River, *1813, copy by Wilhelm Alhorn after the lost original painting*

(Berlin, Nationalgalerie)

Schinkel's "Grand Tour" to Italy

and its impact on the architecture in Berlin and Potsdam

Professor Dr Wolfgang Brönner

Karl Friedrich Schinkel, View of a Country House near Syracuse, Sicily, *1804*

(Berlin, Kupferstichkabinett)

Cornelius Gurlitt, architectural historian and conservator of monuments in Dresden, described in 1900 in his famous "History of Art in the Nineteenth Century" Schinkel's relationship to antiquity as follows: "From his book of travels you can see how little he was touched by Palladio's architecture. No word of joyous affirmation in front of his works in Vicenza, in Venice, no warm lines for Perrault's Louvre, to which Schinkel owed so much for his museum's outline. He was charmed only by the architecture of Hellenic Greece which he had never seen with his own eyes. He had knowledge of the Temples of Paestum and Sicily. He drew the monuments of Pola, Rome, Taormina and Grigenti. But these works did not really capture his spirit. ...." [1]

One wonders what use Schinkel, the classicist, could have made of his Italian experience. We are speaking of the journey which he undertook in 1803 at the age of twenty-two, the first of two journeys to Italy.   This journey led him via Prague and Vienna to Italy, down to Sicily and ended in 1805 with a detour to Paris.   It had the character of the "Grand Tour" of the 18th century, even if Schinkel travelled like a middle-class student on a low budget.

All famous points of great architectural history were included, virtually a complete classical education programme since the renaissance.

Gurlitt sounds almost a little disappointed at Schinkel's lack of interest in these very topics. As far as Schinkel's personal testimony is concerned, everything sounds even more rigorous. There are two very significant letters written by Schinkel in 1804. He writes from Rome in December 1804 to the editor Johann Friedrich Unger:

"During a journey around Italy and its isles I had the opportunity to collect a lot of interesting examples of architecture, to which nobody has paid attention until now. Up to now people have been occupied with exploring thousands of monuments of Greek and Roman antiquity or of the renaissance. … I therefore have no reason to pay attention to these items, particularly as I knew them before and because they do not bring me nearer to the ideal I am pursuing and whose principles I am perhaps going to draw together to form a whole."

And he continues:

"Many buildings dating from the early Middle Ages, even from the time of the Saracen occupation of Sicily, of which a lot of magnificant examples remain, bear the true and ideal character of art and are full of character. Other and more recent works, situated in unknown corners of Italy, cheerfully making use of the landscape in which they are situated and without any regard for the rules of art taught by Palladio, are more characteristic than the majority of that which is produced in Berlin." [2]

The second letter, written in 1804 in Paris, was addressed to his first teacher of architecture, David Gilly. Here we have even more the impression that as far as classical art is concerned, the journey was of no use at all: "The majority of the monuments of antique architecture offer the architect no new ideas because we are familiar with them since our school days. When regarding these works of architecture in reality I feel surprised, not by their greatness but by the picturesque composition of the whole."[3]

It is not clear what Schinkel expected to see when he went to Italy. But it is evident that he was convinced that he already had a wide knowledge of all important items through his theoretical studies in Berlin. His personal experience could only diminish their greatness.   On the other hand, Schinkel

Karl Friedrich Schinkel,
View of Flourishing Greece.
1825, copy by Wilhelm Alhorn
after the lost original painting

(Berlin, Nationalgalerie)

was an attentive and assiduous traveller. He drew unceasingly and even prepared material for future publication . But there were items other than the classical ones which aroused his interest. He did not look for the "rules of Palladio"; he was more interested in the unknown, in products of art and architecture beyond these rules, but full of character, and he looked for the connection of architecture and landscape. He found this in the rural architecture of Italy just as in the works of the Middle Ages which fascinated him again and again. Two drawings may illustrate this. The first one, drawn in 1804, shows the so-called House of the Englishman near Syracuse. The embedding of the rather simple country house architecture in the wildly romantic landscape is one of the basic patterns of his Italian experience.

The second one was drawn in 1806 in Berlin after his return from Italy. It shows an ideal view of the Milan cathedral on a hill above a town. His interest in the architecture of the Middle Ages, articulated again and again during the journey, is manifest. On the other hand, a very special view of the Middle Ages, typical of the 19th century, is looming. The prominent situation of the church on a mountain removes the historical building from its traditional environment and raises it on a pedestal, makes it an exhibition piece.

Other places which Schinkel saw during his journey may have influenced this idea: for instance the Capitol Hill in Rome, the Kryptoportikus of Terracina (which at that time was still believed to be a castle of Theorderich the Great) or the Temples of Segesta and Agrigento. Schinkel made preparations for a publication during his journey. Strictly speaking, it was the publication of architectural details from antiquity and the Middle Ages. His interest was focussed remarkably on the graphical grace of the detail, the decorative ornamentation. He compiled a selection of examples which he wanted to publish when he returned to Berlin. The letter of 1804 to Unger, which I mentioned above, was dedicated to this purpose and was intended to promote this project. But nothing ever became of the publication.

At first glance, the result of Schinkel's first journey to Italy may seem strange but we will   understand it better if we realize who made this journey. Schinkel had just completed his education at the school of architecture in Berlin (founded in 1799) and had been instructed by Gilly, father and son, in the spirit of classicism.   Friedrich Gilly, the son, brilliant and charismatic, was strongly influenced by France and brought many of the ideas of the French revolutionary architecture to Berlin.   Not only the character of the monumental buildings of Boullée but also the utilitarian planning system of Durand were discussed eagerly in Berlin. Schinkel shared a   close friendship with Friedrich Gilly, who was nine years older, and in 1800 when Gilly died at the age of only 28, Schinkel took over his unfinished building projects. Gilly's influence affected not only his interest in the architecture of the Middle Ages (Marienburg), but also in architectural drawing in general.

The classicism which dominated Berlin at that time was fundamentally different from that in France and in England, where the general interest concentrated on Roman antiquity and its modern successors, particularly on the architecture of Andrea Palladio. In Berlin, however, a change loomed at the end of the 18th century. Carl Gotthard Langhans had built the Brandenburger Tor (Brandenburg Gate) (1789-1794), the emphatically Greek character of which was to shine like a beacon for future architecture in Berlin. One felt an affinity with ancient Greece, as Helmut Börsch Supan writes.

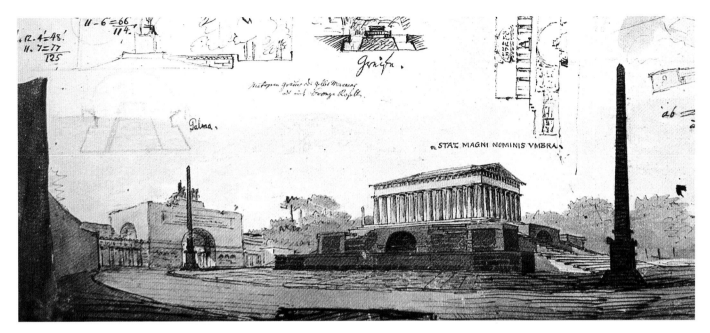

Friedrich Gilly, Project for a Monument to Friedrich the Great, *1797*

(from Rietdorf, Gilly, fig. 43)

Greek antiquity seemed to be much more original, on the other hand it was the Protestant alternative to everything referring to Rome as a model, the French Revolution and the Napoleonic Empire as well as the Roman Catholic Church.[4] Whatever the motivation, architecture in Berlin had already started to pursue an ideal Hellenism before 1800. Schinkel's education at the grammar school in the Grauen Kloster was characterized by Greek enthusiasm. Of major importance for his development as a classical architect was Friedrich Gilly's project of a monument to Friedrich the Great, conceived in 1797 and representing a Dorian peripteral temple above a massive substructure. During his first Italian journey he met Wilhelm von Humboldt in Rome, who also confirmed him in this tendency towards Greece.

Schinkel's second interest was painting. It is probably due to the influence of the congenial Friedrich Gilly that Schinkel did not become a painter or a sculptor. It was Gilly who led him to architecture. Landscape architectures and stage sets form the main part of his pictorial work. His first known drawing, which originated about 1795 or 1798, shows a Greek temple ruin. In 1800 he came forward with an outline for a stage set for *Iphigenie in Aulis* of Euripides, in 1802 for *Iphigenie in Tauris* of Goethe. In contrast to subjects referring to antiquity there are paintings like the *Cathedral on the River* which he did not paint until after his first Italian journey, but which characterizes his view on architecture in general. From very early on he shows a distinctive feeling for architecture in the landscape, which Woltmann later describes as a "genus of the historico-cultural landscape".[5] In addition, he was able to depict ambience and aura and spatial distance in a manner which reminds one of the paintings of Caspar David Friedrich. Schinkel's picturesque view of architecture was to influence the experience of his journey greatly, and was to have a great effect on his future work on his return to Berlin.

The painting which characterizes Schinkel as a painter and architect at the same time, is the famous picture entitled *A View of Flourishing Greece*. It is as good as a programmatic picture allegorizing Schinkel's architectural ideal. It is the programme picture of the *Spreeathen* which came into being at the same time. The term "Spreeathen" (Athens on Spree) had already appeared in

Berlin, The Altes Museum
(Photo Wolfgang Brönner 2000).

1705 in a poem of praise to King Wilhelm I., in which the honoured monarch is equated with the Olympic Jupiter. Architecturally speaking, Berlin did not become the "Spreeathen" until the 19th century.

It needs not confuse us that this picture was not painted until 1823, on the eve of Schinkel's second Italian journey. It is significant for the young Schinkel, too, whose mind was not focussing on romantic temple ruins but on the creative power of antique civilisation. Greece was for him a symbol of the origin and the vitality of culture, with which Man remodels and embellishes Nature. With this idea in his head he scanned Italy, he recorded everything he thought to be creative and primitive, characteristic and void of rules. It was this basic idea which sought affirmation. This affirmation he found in places in Italy very different from those which people travelling before him used to visit. The result of his two Italian journeys is a strengthening of his vision of art and civilisation through the ambience affecting him throughout the country. Schinkel's return to Berlin coincided with Napoleon's defeat of Prussia. So for years there was no basis for architectural activity, until 1810 when he made the acquaintance of the Prussian royal couple. But nobody thought of large and grand buildings. Nevertheless, important products emerged in three different fields of art: in painting, like the Cathedral by the Water, stage designs, and in applied arts (for instance some furniture for the Queen, models for cast iron plates for instance and in architecture (the porticus of the mausoleum for Queen Louise, 1810). But the most impressive result of his first Italian journey is the cultural landscape of Potsdam, which he developed with the royal landscape gardener Peter Joseph Lenné and which after Schinkel's death was completed by King Friedrich Wilhelm IV. and Schinkel's pupil Ludwig Persius. In 1824 he started his second Italian journey, this time at the special command of the King. He had been commissioned to build a new museum in front of the Royal Palace in Berlin, known today as the "Altes Museum".

Accompanied by the art historian Gustav Friedrich Waagen, Schinkel travelled around continental Europe, most of the time being spent in Italy in order to visit many examples of this building type. As the journey was mainly dedicated to this purpose, it was anything but an educational tour. However, impressions were refreshed and intensified en route, mainly in Rome. In contrast to his first journey, Schinkel was now interested in antique architecture and its renaissance followers. This time he seems to see Rome from a different angle. But we should be careful when remembering his words during his first Italian journey. There was no real lack of interest at that time. In my opinion, his words, quoted at the beginning of this lecture, do not indicate exactly what he felt; I think that they reveal much more a superimposition of new and unexpected impressions which caught him, a candid and open nature, unprepared. During the second journey he opened his mind more to the antique remains and broadened his view of Italy.

During this second journey Schinkel visited Paestum for the first time. We note that he was specially affected by the most elegant of the temples, the so-called Temple of Neptune (Hera II), as well by the details of the building as a whole, and finally by the combination of architecture and landscape. This way Italy was again a source from which he took his inspiration. Everything he saw, the picturesque farmhouses in the landscape, the medieval churches, the temples of Paestum and Sicily and the town and landscapes were dominated in his mind by the aura of a Greek ideal he had never seen previously, as we know: the ideal of character and originality, of harmony, fortitude and morality.

Consequently, the impact of this journey is multifarious.[6] But even the classical buildings he constructed, bear few evident and immediate references to any great Italian experience noted during his journeys. Let us turn first to the New Guardhouse Unter den

Berlin, The New Guardhouse on the Unter den Linden. (Photo Kurt Gawlitta 2008)

Berlin, The Theatre at Gendarmenmarkt (Photo Kurt Gawlitta 2008)

Potsdam, Sanssouci, The Charlottenhof Castle.
(Photo Wolfgang Pfauder, Stiftung Preußische Schlösser und Gärten Berlin-Brandenburg)

Potsdam, Sanssouci, Roman Bath.
(Photo Hagen Immel, Stiftung Preußische Schlösser und Gärten Berlin-Brandenburg)

Linden (1816), to which a Doric temple porticus adds the character of martial severity. The porticus of the guardhouse is situated in front of a mere cube, typical of Palladian villas, but the emphasis on the simple solids recalls French revolutionary architecture.

The new theatre at the Gendarmenmarkt (1818-21) is again a porticus in front of a cubical body, or rather, a body composed of cubes. Despite its monumentality this building is light and elegant. This second building is obviously influenced by Palladian architecture, too. But at the same time French architecture, especially Durand's Cours d'architecture of 1805, is predominant as far as the clear grouping of architectural bodies is concerned.

The following two buildings were erected immediately after his second journey to Italy.

At first he built the small Charlottenhof Castle in the Park of Sanssouci (begun in 1825) Again a portico is situated in front of a cube, but this time with very light and elegant proportions. Near by and as a part of Charlottenhof, Schinkel built the Roman bath, a group of buildings combining the Italian farmhouse and the Pompeian villa. These constructions are the principal items of the cultural landscape, the Prussian arcadia at Potsdam, which has meanwhile become part of the World Heritage List (together with Sanssouci and the New Palace).

Schinkel's main architectural work, the so-called "Altes Museum" in the palace square in Berlin, was constructed 1825-28. The temple, reduced to one front collonade on a high base, reminds one of the colonnade of the Nouveau Louvre of Perrault, which he saw in 1804. The interior of the central dome undoubtedly originates from the Pantheon, but from the outside it is hidden to the visitor coming from the palace square. The empty space in front of the museum underlines the monumentality of the simple row of columns. The temples of Segesta and Agrigento, situated alone in the landscape which Schinkel had seen twenty-four years before, may well have had a late effect. Schinkel's impact on the urban development of Berlin was no less important. Let us concentrate on the surroundings of the new museum in the centre of Berlin, the so-called "Schlossinsel" (Palace Island). It is the place where the famous avenue Unter den Linden ends, the palace yard.   At the other end of the Unter den Linden stands the Brandenburg Gate. Opposite the museum stood the grand Royal Palace, built in the 17th century by Anreas Schlüter, and between these buildings was the wide space of the palace square which up to the construction of the museum had mainly been used as a parade ground. Schinkel's planning concentrated on this area. He developed an urban space in which the Royal Palace was no longer the centre of the city. The new focal point was now a group of buildings, consisting of the Royal Palace, the new museum and the cathedral of the middle of the 18th century. It is easy to recognize that there is a socio-political reason which influenced this plan. And we are not surprised to hear that this unofficial plan did not meet with King Friedrich Wilhelm VI.'s approval, who drew up his own plan, placing a great new cathedral in the middle of the place.

The impression of a social-reformatory idea was intensified by the planning of a new bridge from the avenue Unter den Linden to the palace square. It was to be decorated with a sequence of sculptures representing Victories and Heroes. Strictly speaking, they are allegories of the struggle for freedom against Napoleon, and of the citizen doing his duty towards society. The hero suffering for the idea he pursues was - under the influence of the king - replaced by warriors in attack as a symbol of state power. Nevertheless, the whole of this urban restructuring shows – even today - that Schinkel followed the idea of a new society which was influenced by an Hellenistic ideal and which was to gather together all social strengths.[7]

The outline of a princely residence, which is part of Schinkel's material for an unfinished textbook on architecture, may help our understanding of this. The picture from 1835 reveals the complex structure of its architecture and its functions which he thought to be accommodated in an ideal city:

Schlossbrücke, Berlin, The Castle Bridge at the end of the Unter den Linden. (Photo c.1930)

- An urban centre, prospering through commerce and trade, situated besides a river or near the sea and surrounded by fertile soil.
- A summer and a winter residence for the princely family
- Some covered fairgrounds
- A meeting place for scientists and artists
- A library connected with the meeting place
- A collection of sculptures
- A collection of antiquities
- A collection of natural history

Of course, it is an ideal vision but Schinkel tried to realize it to some extent in the centre of Berlin. Italy again supplied the architectural models. The cathedral,   which was to confine the palace square to the north, was to be embellished with a dome taken from the Pantheon; the inspiration for the the new bridge with its statues leading from the avenue Unter den Linden to the palace square derives from the Bridge of Angels in Rome, because Victories were also placed there in Roman times just as in Berlin now.

From the great number of architects travelling to Italy at that time I will mention only two, whose lives were somewhat close to Schinkel's: Friedrich Weinbrenner and Leo von Klenze.

Friedrich Weinbrenner, born in 1766 in Karlsruhe, was late starting his career as an architect. His education led him from Vienna to Dresden and finally in 1791 to Berlin. The few months he spent there, under the influence of Carl Gotthard Langhans, who built the Brandenburg Gate, and David Gilly, father of the famous Friedrich Gilly, had a lasting effect because he began to inform himself about antique architecture in general and about Palladianism. After his stay in Berlin in 1792 he travelled to Italy, only six years after Goethe and eleven years before Schinkel, where he visited Paestum. The landscapes he drew, the farmhouses and the Temples at Paestum, are reminiscent of Schinkel's pictures of farmhouses and of Agrigento and Segesta. Like Schinkel he preferred the so-called Temple of Neptune.

Under the influence of the French revolutionary architecture he developed an austere and spartan style of architecture, very different from Schinkel's svelte and light constructions. On the other hand, he was also affected by the picturesque and irregular Italian farmhouse architecture.

Leo von Klenze belongs to Schinkel's generation. His father sent him to Berlin to study law, but under the influence of Friedrich Gilly he changed to architecture. So it is not surprising that he, like Schinkel, adored Greek architecture. He was a very good painter. The placement of architecture in the landscape was of great importance for him; in Italy he drew Italian farmhouses and medieval buildings with the same ardour. But his interest in antiquity is subtly different from Schinkel's. His first Italian journey, which he started at almost the same time as Schinkel, was interrupted in order to take on a position in Kassel. This was followed by a move to Munich where he became royal architect in 1820, and thus Schinkel's south German counterpart. In 1824, in the same year as Schinkel, he visited Paestum, when he accompanied the Bavarian crown prince. Like Weinbrenner and Schinkel he was most impressed

**Professor
Dr Wolfgang Brönner**

Studied Law at Wurzburg, Lausanne and Bonn, followed by studies in History of Art and Classical Archaeology at Bonn. He has been professionally involved in heritage conservation and in 1991 became Director for the Conservation of Monuments in the Rheinland Palatinate. His main interest in art history is focused on the art and architecture of the 19th century in Germany.

by the classical Neptune Temple. It was to have a long-lasting fascination for him, as is demonstrated in a painting after 1859. Furthermore, Klenze is fascinated by romantic ruins and the reconstruction of antique scenes, like this one of ancient Athens. His idea of Greek antiquity, the original stones of which he knew better than Schinkel because he visited Greece in 1834, was concentrated much more on the real remains of this culture than on the social ideal. And his occupation with Greek antiquity was much more archeological, as the many drawings of details and site measurings which he carried out in Italy and Greece can prove.

As we see, Schinkel was not bound to a specific style of architecture and he had a very pragmatic approach to history. But it was a general classical view of mankind which dominated. It was a projection of the Greek political system onto the rising bourgeois community of the 19th century. His classical architecture is therefore a transformation of a primitive idea into a world of grace and refinement. Above all, the towns and landscapes he saw in Italy and the people he met there, supplied him with the aura and the way of life, which was to pervade the new world he imagined.

Due to his great authority Berlin was for a long time only marginally touched by the rising historicism. The change did not come about until the 1880s when the architectural schools of Hanover and Munich caused a stir and gradually eroded the Hellenistic influence of the school of Schinkel.

1   Cornelius Gurlitt, Die deutsche Kunst des neunzehnten Jahrhunderts. Ihr Ziele und ihre Thaten. Berlin 1900, S. 75 f.

2   Karl Friedrich Schinkel, Reisen nach Italien. Ed. Gottfried Riemann, Berlin / Weimar 1994, Erste Reise 1803-1805, S. 220 f., 260

3   Ibid., S. 230, 260

4   Helmut Börsch-Supan, Griechisches und Römisches bei Schinkel. In: PreußenJahrBuch. Berlin 2001, S. 106-109

5   Alfred Woltmann, Aus vier Jahrhunderten niederländisch-deutscher Kunstgeschichte. Berlin 1878, Schinkel als Maler, S. 191-270, 195

6   Martin Steffens, Karl Friedrich Schinkel 1781-18441, an Architect in the Service of Beauty. Köln 2003

7   Peter Springer, Schinkels Schlossbrücke in Berlin. Zweckbau und Monument. Frankfurt am Main / Berlin / Wien 1981

Architecture of the Antique

The enduring legacy of Sir John Soane

Margaret Richardson

The Breakfast Room, No 13 Lincoln's Inn Fields, 1812-13. Coloured light enters the room at either end of the central canopy dome.

(By courtesy of the Trustees of Sir John Soane's Museum. Photo: Martin Charles)

At 5 o'clock in the morning on 18th March 1778 Soane set out for Italy, with the first quarterly payment of £30 from his Royal Academy scholarship, and travelling expenses of a similar sum, in his pocket. With him was Robert Furze Brettingham, relying on an allowance from his father. For Soane the date was momentous, frequently to be recollected in his notebooks over the years: it was the most important event in his life.

They reached Rome on 2nd May and set about visiting, drawing and measuring the antique buildings. He went to Tivoli, where he measured the circular Temple of Vesta, as well as to Pompeii, Terracina and Paestum – and later to Sicily. He returned to England in mid 1780, slightly earlier than he had planned, led on by the promise from the unreliable Bishop of Derry that he should build a mansion at Ickworth, which sadly came to nothing.

Before he left for Rome, Sir William Chambers had given him a copy of a letter which he had written earlier to a former pupil, Edward Stevens, who was then in Rome. It contained advice about what he should study. Chambers wrote that he should "draw, measure and observe everything upon the spot yourself – always see with your own eyes ...and form, if you can a style of your own, in which you should endeavour to avoid the faults and blend the perfections of all". This advice echoed that of Piranesi's who had written in 1769 that "an artist, who would do himself honour, must not content himself with copying faithfully the ancients, but studying their works he ought to show himself of an inventive, and, I had almost said, of a creating Genius".

Soane certainly took Chambers's advice to heart in developing that highly idiosyncratic approach to design which was to be recognised as the "Soane style". And there were certain buildings in Italy which greatly influenced his approach.

There was the primitivism of the Doric temples at Paestum and the unorthodox character of the Temple of Vesta at Tivoli with its unusual order, its comparatively plain architrave and its curving peristyle of columns which produced that picturesque "variety of light and shadow" which Soane admired. There was also the Pantheon, with its brilliant lighting effects, and above all, perhaps, Hadrian's Villa which displayed Roman architects' handling of domes and groin-vaulting. More than any other buildings in Rome, these domed spaces were to have a profound influence on Soane.

The interior domes, or canopies, of Soane's buildings came to form one of the basic themes in his design and became the most influential in the 20th century. In his Royal Academy lectures Soane had criticised modern domes – for example the dome of St Paul's – because they "seemed to be placed on roofs without any visible support and without apparent connection with the other parts of the edifices". In contrast, as he said, "the domes of the ancients seem always to grow out of the substructure and to Harmonize with it in the most gradual and pleasing manner forming, as it were, a canopy to the entire edifice". He might have been describing the Temple of Canopus at Hadrian's Villa, which is scalloped with concavities to form an umbrella-like vault.

Soane's Drawing Room at Wimpole Hall, of 1790, is the first realization of his transformation of the traditional Renaissance dome into a "canopy" – a word he always used. At Wimpole he removes the intermediate storey formed by the arches and pendentives so that the canopy dome springs directly from the walls of the room. The arches are still necessary to the structure and are sliced out of its spherical surface.

Engraving, by G.B.Piranesi, of the Temple of Canopus at Hadrian's Villa at Tivoli near Rome; a building which displayed Roman architects' handling of domes at its most inventive.

(Sir John Soane's Museum)

Later, in 1813, he perfected his canopy dome in his own Breakfast Room at Lincoln's Inn Fields. As Soane was to write: "In the centre rises a spherical ceiling, springing from four segmental arches supported by the same number of pilasters, forming a rich canopy. The views from the room into the Monument Court and into the Museum, the mirrors in the ceiling and the looking glasses, combined with the variety of outline and general arrangement in the design and decoration of this limited space present an almost infinite succession of those fanciful effects which constitute "the poetry of architecture". These are Soane's words but one should add that the room is a rectangle: the canopy dome defines the central square but at either end concealed lantern lights allow light – coloured light - to enter the room. This feature was adopted by several architects at the end of the 20th century, as we shall see.

Soane himself repeated the theme of Soane's Breakfast Room on several occasions – for example in the 1818 Dividend Office at the Bank of England, he has all but removed the walls in the central area. And at the Freemasons' Hall the support for the canopy has disappeared, leaving four hanging lamps to indicate where the structure may have been.

Soane died in 1837, having previously negotiated a private Act of Parliament in 1833, which left his house and museum to the care of Trustees of his own choosing. He intended his building to benefit the general public and particularly students and "amateurs". The Curators were also in the future to keep the house and museum "as nearly as circumstances would admit in the state in which he had left it".

After his death Soane had very few followers. Shortly after he died Thomas Donaldson, the Hon. Secretary of the newly formed Institute of British Architects, read a paper on Soane and his achievements: it was, in effect, a memorial address, but a strange one. He praised him as a Benefactor of the Institute but was openly critical about certain aspects of his architecture, saying that many of the elevations of his early houses were deficient in taste, particularly in his unorthodox way of handling the orders. He was full of praise for the exterior of the Bank but referred to the "many aberrations of genius" in the interiors. He also admitted that many of the works of Soane's later years, like Chelsea Hospital, the Law Courts and the Freemasons' Hall, all had "the same peculiar defects".

This then was the official summing up of Soane's career by an arch-establishment member of the profession: Soane was to be praised for his actions as a Benefactor, for his work as a Professor of Architecture, for the generosity of his gift to the nation of his house and museum, but not for his architecture which was judged to be "peculiar", personal and given to novelties. And Donaldson was not alone in these opinions, he was simply giving voice to the many criticisms of so-called eccentricities which Soane had borne throughout his career.

So what was the immediate legacy of his work? Both John Foulston and George Wightwick often adopted the stripped facades, the incised ornament and the domed interior spaces in Plymouth, and Wightwick himself, who had worked briefly for Soane as his Secretary, wrote a wonderful piece about his time in the office. He wrote that "it seems to have been his aim to unite the classic delicacies of Greek and Roman design with the playfulness of Gothic – not by the use of the pointed arch – but by adopting the principle of continuous lines ramifying from the vertical into the circular." Wightwick's insight into Soane's work is remarkable for its day and predates any other analysis of the primitive qualities of his style by more than a century.

Several of Soane's pupils, notably John Sanders, Francis Edwards and David Mocatta, continued another aspect of Soane's architecture – the abstracted brick classicism of Chelsea Hospital and Dulwich Picture Gallery which had so outraged his contemporaries. Sanders' Duke of York Headquarters in Chelsea, Edwards' Lion Breweries and Mocatta's buildings for the London, Brighton and South Coast line were all of stock brick and had the dignified, functional simplicity of early Victorian architecture.

After Soane's death Cockerell stepped neatly into his shoes, both as Professor of Architecture at the Royal Academy and as Architect to the Bank, but had, however, scarcely a kind word to say about his predecessor. He found much to criticize in Soane's Bank and in 1848 destroyed the austere line of Soane's acroteria along the parapets by substituting a massive balustrade. In his diaries, Cockerell wrote of the Law Courts in 1826, "thought them trivial, absurd in their architecture. Should not expect to hear sense in such foolish rooms."

There were a few lone voices in praise of Soane – notably Richard Brown

(Pictures on pages 148, 149, 150 and 151 are reproduced from the Royal Academy Catalogue *John Soane Architect: Master of Space and Light*, 1999, edited by Margaret Richardson and Mary Anne Steven)

J.M.Gandy's view of the interior of Dulwich Picture Gallery, 1823. Dulwich has been one of the most important prototypes for the art gallery in the Western World.

(Sir John Soane's Museum)

and John Weale, but times had changed and originality, particularly Soane's kind of personal originality, could hardly find favour in the period dominated by the Gothic Revival and Ruskin.

Soane's name, however, was kept alive throughout the 19th century by references to the Bank of England and to his Museum at Lincoln's Inn Fields. Most found reason to praise the Bank which left a legacy of another kind in establishing a grand prototype, not in a specific stylistic sense, but rather for commercial buildings in general. Many banks followed Soane's precedent for single-storey buildings with blind exteriors and interiors lit by skylights above domes. And the Museum was universally liked for its eccentricities, curiosities and picturesque arrangements, rather than for its architecture.

Then during the first two decades of the 20th century a reassessment of Soane was brought about by the revival of classicism. This in turn led to such influential books as Albert Richardson's 1914 *Monumental Classic Architecture in Great Britain and Ireland*, which was unusual in the full-blown praise he lavished on the Bank and on Soane – saying that he was the most original architect of the 18th century.

Richardson had led the way but it was really in the 1920s that Soane became the generally admired architect that he is today. And it was the somewhat unlikely figure of Roger Fry who first drew public attention to the primitivist qualities in Soane's work in a controversial lecture delivered on 19th May 1921 at the RIBA. Fry had by then become the English spokesman for Modernism and abstract form in painting, and also had decided views on architecture, detesting what he called "the archaeological humbug of the historical-revival styles that typified so much Victorian and Edwardian architecture." He thought that architects did not make much of the possible play of elementary plastic forms and most of his lecture also inveighed against useless ornament. As he said "To my mind there has been little architecture of outstanding merit in this country since the end of the 18th century. Sir John Soane who built the Bank of England and Dulwich Picture Gallery is, with one or two exceptions, the only architect since then whose work is tolerable."

This stirred up a good deal of controversy. *The Times* covered the lecture extensively in interviews with John Simpson, Fry and Sir Reginald Blomfield, who, as one would expect, disagreed strongly with Fry and particularly with

Fry's praise of Soane, saying that Soane had "a mischievous passion for original design." Fry's lecture had, however, caused a good deal of public discussion and had drawn Soane's name into the arena of Modernism for the first time.

The dreadful destruction and demolition of the Bank in the 1920s, which caused widespread debate at a time when there was no Georgian Group, also had the effect of publicising Soane's architecture as well as his reputation. The splendid black and white photographs of the Bank, taken by Frank Yerbury before its destruction, were published widely in the national and architectural press and also served as the plates for a new book on Soane in 1925 by an architect of the younger generation, Harry Birnstingl. He was an architect who had trained at the Architectural Association and who was aware of contemporary thinking in architecture. He was the first to see Soane as "the first modern English architect. For that which distinguishes modern architecture arises from enhanced self-consciousness, from the powers of reasoning and adaptation; powers acting as often to its own detriment as to its good. And these qualities Soane possessed." Henry

Russell Hitchcock also included Soane as a precursor in his early *Modern Architecture*, 1929, recognising him as "unquestionably the greatest architect of the beginning of the 19th century", and as an architect, "working with space, and even with light, for effects of abstract form."

Consequently, by the time of the centenary of Soane's death in 1937, Soane's reputation was firmly established as one of the greatest English architects. *The Times* accorded him a third leader written by John Summerson, his first piece on Soane: "In John Soane British architecture can claim a man of very great imaginative power whose work has a value of a kind which opinion ascribes readily enough to the English poets, but less readily to the architects."

During the second half of the 20th century Soane's architecture slowly came to have a greater influence on the work of contemporary architects. In the 1960s

Philip Johnson, The Guest House at the Philip Johnson Residence, New Canaan, Connecticut, USA, 1953.
In making his dome of canvas, Johnson echoes the lightness of Soane's Breakfast Room canopy.

(New York: Ezra Stoller © Esto)

architecture began to move away from the orthodox handling of form dictated by the Modern Movement towards a more complex manipulation of space and light. This tendency is well represented in Robert Venturi's *Complexity and Contradiction in Architecture* of 1966. Venturi took the well-known

Philip Johnson, The Kneses Tifereth Israel Synagogue, Port Chester, New York, USA, 1956.
In this design Johnson alludes to Soane's motif of hanging arches in his Court of Chancery.

(New York: Ezra Stoller © Esto)

rooms in the form of suspended arches, the intricacies of planning and of spaces within spaces and the layering of canopies and domes.

From the 1960s onwards Soane's architecture has been used for inspiration rather than direct imitation, although many architects have acknowledged both the No 13 Breakfast Room and Dulwich Picture Gallery as direct sources for their designs.

Philip Johnson, however, is an earlier example of an architect experimenting with Soanean "ambiguities". He was a close friend of Henry Russell Hitchcock and made two visits with him to the Museum in the 1950s. Soane's influence can be seen in the canopy inside his 1953 Guest House at New Canaan and in his 1956 Synagogue at Port Chester, New York, to which Summerson referred in a letter to Dorothy Stroud in 1968. Summerson wrote "Last night I did my "Soanean space" stuff and it went rather well because everybody recognised without being told that Philip Johnsonian space is the same as Soanean space and that in fact his synagogue is some sort of paraphrase of the Court of Chancery." As Franz Schulze wrote in his biography of

Miesian jingle "less is more" and replaced it with "less is a bore" and he looked for ambiguities and complexities in the architecture of the past and present that would reinforce an architecture of richness and meaning. And he found as many complexities in the work of such historical figures as Soane,

Hawksmoor and Lutyens as he did in the work of Le Corbusier, Aalto and Kahn. The book echoed one aspect of contemporary thinking and had a considerable influence. Venturi drew attention to many of those qualities in Soane's work: the complex combination of shapes in his ceilings, the partition of spaces in

Johnson: "A generation younger than Ledoux and a generation older than Schinkel, Soane was another of the great 18th century to 19th century classicists Philip had made a special point of admiring. He was also the most idiosyncratic of the three. In the past Philip had preferred the soberer formality of Ledoux and Schinkel, but now, perhaps in consequence of his search for new forms, he found Soane's eccentricity especially appropriate to the faintly decadent mood he wished to evoke in the Guest House. Yet what made that remodelled space appear most radical by the standards of 1953 was Philip's candid use of arch and dome, historical forms that had been universally discarded by the modernists, especially by those close to the International Style."

During the Post-Modern era of the late 1970s and 80s there have been many reflections of Soanean themes in the work of a generation of architects encouraged once more in their architectural schools to seek out imaginative historical references.

From the 1970s the Soane Museum became a teaching resource for architectural tutors from all over the world, a place where their students were encouraged to study the handling of light, the canopy and star-fish ceilings and the vertical and horizontal extensions of space. And the references to Soane's work became international although I can only mention a few in this paper.

Arata Isozaki's architecture shows the dialogue between contemporary Japanese culture and western architecture at its most complex. He presents these western sources as self-contained "quotations" – for example he inserted a version of Soane's Breakfast Room in his Vories Hall in Tokyo, designed in 1987. He had been so fascinated by the Breakfast Room that he wrote a book about the Museum which was published in 1983. In it he wrote: "Although the Museum is more original than the work of Soane's contemporaries, it shares a common characteristic with them: the selective adoption of classical architectural language which was the foundation of his early career. We see in this Museum how such architecture could be freely and elegantly composed so as to deviate from the paradigm of the day. It reminds us that only such deviation can advance various investigations which reach beyond the limits of an era".

Two Spanish architects have also incorporated Soanean forms into their work. In 1984 Juan Navarro Baldeweg, who is a great admirer of Soane,

Arata Isozaki, Vories Hall, Tokyo, 1987.
The use of the 'quotation' of Soane's Breakfast Room to emphasize the meeting of East and West.

(Tokio: Tomio Ohasi)

Opposite: Rafael Moneo, Atocha Station, Madrid, 1990s.
Here Moneo evokes the external forms of Soane's canopy domes.

(Barcelona: Duccio Malagamba)

designed a suspended canopy for an auditorium in a cultural centre in Murcia, a prototype for his 1985 Congress Hall at Salamanca, where the dome has the same dimensions as that of the Pantheon in Rome. Rafael Moneo is also an admirer of Soane and has used Soane's canopy dome in different forms – in his 1998 Library in the Cultural Centre, Don Benito, Badajoz in Spain and for the more unusual public use at the Atocha Station in Madrid. Oswald Mathias Ungers adapted the theme of a building within a building in his 1983 design for his Architecture Museum in Frankfurt, where the

Right: Juan Navarro Baldeweg, Congress Hall, Salamanca, Spain, 1985-92.
A reinterpretation of Soane's Breakfast Room as a suspended ceiling in reinforced concrete.

(Barcelona: Duccio Malagamba)

Richard MacCormac, New Court, Fitzwilliam College, Cambridge, 1987. Above: Bays, with concrete columns and entablatures, evoke the second floor projecting bay on the facade of the Soane Museum.

Right: The sense of enclosure within one of the bays, evoking the alcove on the second floor of the Soane Museum.

(MJP Architects, both images)

temple form at the top of the Museum has been likened to the free-standing Student's Room at the back of the Soane.

In their National Gallery extension of 1985 – 91 Robert Venturi and Denise Scott Brown openly admit their debt to Dulwich Picture Gallery and particularly to its enfilade of arches and ceiling forms which create an aura of natural light in the galleries.

Richard MacCormac has a deep knowledge of Soane's work and, like Venturi, is able to interpret the forms and layered spaces of Soane's buildings in abstract terms. Many of these have been creatively evoked, but not necessarily literally imitated, in his own buildings. For example, the elevations of New Court at Fitzwilliam College, Cambridge, of 1987, are defined by a series of aedicule-like projecting bays, symmetrically arranged on either side of each entrance. These bays, with pre-cast concrete columns and entablatures, stand outside the student rooms giving a wonderful sense of enclosure from within. MacCormac has likened them to the way in which the stone façade of Soane's house stands in front of the brick construction behind, creating a small internal balcony space on the second floor.

But by far the greatest influence on MacCormac has been the inspiration of Soane's spatial and lighting effects. He has said of the Breakfast Room at Lincoln's Inn Fields: "Here the shallow vault defines the expected space but this has been extended by walls placed beyond the limits of the dome. The house is full of such tricks which keep offering unexpected extensions of space." And just as coloured light enters the room above these walls, so in MacCormac's Fitzwilliam Chapel, of 1992, light floods down the curved inner walls from a hidden source.

Perhaps the most learned of MacCormac's buildings in his career so far is the Garden Quadrangle at St John's College, Oxford, of 1990-91. The towers of the residential buildings evoke the Elizabethan prospect towers at Hardwick Hall, but the most exciting spaces are those below the raised terraces which demonstrate his love of complexity. On either side of a central, circular atrium, which is open to the sky like a Piranesi ruin, are a sunken auditorium to the West and a Dining room to the East, both with shallow domes and pendentives which are conscious references to Soane.

Richard MacCormac, Auditorium, St John's College, Oxford, 1990-91. The shallow dome and pendentives are conscious references to Soane's Breakfast Room.

(MJP Architects)

Richard MacCormac, Southwark Tube Station, London, late 1990s.
The interior shows the influence of Soane's use of coloured light.

(MJP Architects)

Margaret Richardson OBE FSA

Former Director of Sir John Soane Museum from 1995 to 2005 following an earlier career as Assistant Curator at the RIBA Drawings Collection from 1963. She hasspecialised in the architecture of the Art and Crafts Movement and 20th century architecture, and is now the Honorary Curator of Architecture at the Royal Academy.

Soane's use of coloured light, as well as the influence of the space and light artist, James Turrell, who is, in turn very interested in the Soane Museum, inspired MacCormac to create his "big blue space" in the Wellcome Wing at the Science Museum in 1997. His intention was to create an interior which had the "cool blue radiance of a night sky to induce a sense of elation and wonder" – the 18th century's sense of the sublime – a sensation he also created at Southwark Tube station on the Jubilee Line.

The influence of Soane's architecture continues in the 21st century and, in the present decade, perhaps the greatest interest is in the way Soane handles light and lighting effects. Soane's ability to continue to engage the attention of architects working today, without inhibiting their powers of invention, is possibly his greatest legacy.

This lecture was based on my essay on *Soane's Legacy*, with extracts from Christopher Woodward's essay on *Soane's 'Designs for Domes'*, both in the Royal Academy's Catalogue *John Soane Architect: Master of Space and Light*, 1999, edited by Margaret Richardson and Mary Anne Stevens.

I am grateful to Peter Sawbridge at the Royal Academy of Arts for allowing me to use the material in the RA Catalogue; to Sir Richard MacCormac and Richard Robinson of MJP Architects and to Susan Palmer at Sir John Soane's Museum.

Margaret Richardson

EUROPA NOSTRA

ABOUT EUROPA NOSTRA

Europa Nostra, the pan European Federation for Cultural Heritage, is the representative platform of over 250 heritage NGOs active in 45 countries across Europe. It is the voice of this vast movement of European civil society active in the field of heritage towards international bodies concerned, in particular the European Union Institutions, the Council of Europe and UNESCO.

Europa Nostra is dedicated to putting heritage and its benefits in the mainstream of public consciousness and to making heritage a priority for public policies both at European and national levels. Its specific objectives are to promote, at a European level, high standards of quality in the fields of heritage conservation, architecture, urban and rural planning and to advocate a balanced and sustainable development of urban and rural, built and natural environment.

Europa Nostra supports national and international campaigns for the preservation and rescue of Europe's heritage at risk. It encourages exemplary initiatives in favour of the conservation and enhancement of cultural heritage by recognising outstanding heritage achievements, in particular through the running of the European Union Prize for Cultural Heritage / Europa Nostra Awards. In 2006 and 2007, Europa Nostra acted as the Liaison Office for the coordination of the European Heritage Days, a joint action of the Council of Europe and the European Commission.

Through its various activities, Europa Nostra seeks to highlight the importance of cultural heritage as a building block of European identity and as a contribution to the strengthening of the sense of European citizenship.

www.europanostra.org